16

bbg

UNIVERSITY OF CHICAGO STUDIES IN LIBRARY SCIENCE

The Medium-sized Public Library: Its Status and Future

The Medium-sized
Public Library
Its Status and Future

The Twenty-seventh Annual Conference
of the Graduate Library School
August 8–10, 1962

Edited by LEON CARNOVSKY and HOWARD W. WINGER

 THE UNIVERSITY OF CHICAGO PRESS

The papers in this volume were published originally in the
LIBRARY QUARTERLY, *January 1963*

TABLE OF CONTENTS

INTRODUCTION

"T HE Medium-sized Public Library: Its Status and Future" was the topic of the Twenty-seventh Annual Conference of the Graduate Library School, August 8–10, 1962. The ten papers presented at the Conference are here reproduced.

In spite of the emphasis on library systems in American Library Association standards, the position of the medium-sized library—arbitrarily defined as one serving a local population of between 25,000 and 150,000—remains solidly entrenched and is likely to remain as a basic reality in the pattern of American public librarianship. Its problems differ from those of the village and small-town library, on the one hand, and of the metropolitan, county, and regional library, on the other. Because of its importance in the general fabric of local and state government and because of its significance in contributing to the material and cultural welfare of its community, it deserves the concern of librarian and social scientist alike.

What is the medium-sized community like? In 1929 the Lynds published their classic portrait of Middletown, a study that stimulated numerous other investigations by social anthropologists and sociologists. But no community remains static, and it is to describe the character of "Middletown" today that the first paper of this Conference was devoted. Along with its sociological aspect is the financial: what is happening to the collection and expenditure of the tax dollar, and what seem to be future trends? How does the medium-sized community fare in the competition for tax funds, and what are the prospects of the several public agencies in the quest for their share?

Against this background, the Conference turned to a consideration of the public library itself. Following a delineation of the medium-sized library, its distribution and major characteristics, certain aspects are selected for extended analysis. What impact does the library make in its service to children and young people? To adults? How, if at all, has the lush growth of paperback publication affected the demand for library books? What is the obligation of the library to adult education, and what types of adult-education programs seem most appropriate? Has the recent increase in school libraries led to a diminution in public library use—or is any effect at all discernible?

1

Other areas command attention—the development and limitations in building book collections in view of community characteristics and financial resources, trends in book costs and book appropriations, the never absent specter of censorship, and the role of the library board in setting and supporting a book selection policy. Also, since many libraries are faced with the necessity of planning new buildings, or of transforming an old one to meet increased or changed responsibilities, one paper considered the role of the consultant in solving the numerous problems involved. And since technological developments are exerting an influence on social institutions, questions were raised about their relation to the medium-sized public library. Can such developments reduce routine operations? Are they likely to affect the use of personnel, and perhaps even contribute to the solution of the crucial problem of personnel shortages?

Finally, the Conference turned to a consideration of the place of the medium-sized public library in the larger system, with particular reference to New York, where substantial state grants have been provided to facilitate "systems" development. The changes that have come about throughout the state, and particularly the degree to which the medium-sized library has been responsible for them, are explored realistically.

It is with pleasure and gratitude that we acknowledge the assistance of the Joseph Fels Foundation, Inc., in making this Conference possible.

LEON CARNOVSKY
HOWARD W. WINGER
Directors of the Conference

THE MIDDLE-SIZED AMERICAN CITY AT MID-CENTURY

PETER H. ROSSI

MIDDLE-SIZED cities (defined in this paper as cities with populations between 25,000 and 100,000) have a special place in the hearts of Americans. Even the ambivalence with which they are regarded expresses the importance that we have given to the middle-sized city in American life. The middle-sized city is regarded both with affection and with disdain. In American mythology, "back home" is a city around 50,000, the typical locale for sentimental movies set in the period around the turn of the century. We also see the middle-sized community as the home of philistinism, the recruiting ground for the American Legion, and the locale for poor taste in journalism, the fine arts, and education. "Peoria" gets as many laughs as "Brooklyn" on the audience-participation shows.

It is therefore not surprising that the classic American community study is of Muncie, Indiana—"Middletown." (In contrast, the English can point to Booth's *Life and Labour of the People in London*.)[1] To capture the essence of American culture and institutions, the Lynds chose Muncie, Indiana, because its middle-ness in size, economic base, demographic composition promised to provide an appropriate setting for the assessment of America in the post-World War I period. The Lynds brought to their task extraordinary skill and sensitivity, and the popularity of their

work is a credit in large part to their competence. But there is more to the success of the Middletown books than the skills of the authors alone. In the first half of the twentieth century, we felt that America was more properly represented by Muncie than by the teeming urban centers or the declining rural areas. New York and Chicago were still too foreign in population and flavor, while the farm and the countryside were so obviously being decanted into the urban areas. H. L. Mencken's "booboisie" were still small city folk, and Sinclair Lewis' "Zenith" was yet to grow into a metropolis. The urban novel and the sociology of the metropolis had to wait until the second quarter of this century to develop.

It is now almost forty years since the Lynds did their field work for the first Middletown book. Muncie was roaring through the twenties then. When the Lynds returned for their second stint a decade later, the town was in the throes of the Great Depression. Except for an occasional journalistic foray reported in the pages of the popular magazines, Muncie has slipped into a comparative oblivion. Certainly sociologists and anthropologists have neglected to bring the town's social science chronicle up to date.

The center of gravity of social science interest has shifted to the metropolis since World War II. We have come to recognize that large cities are a permanent feature of our physical and social landscapes and that more and more of

[1] Ed. C. B. Booth (9 vols.; London: Macmillan Co., 1892–97).

3

our population will be living in the major metropolitan centers. It even looked for a while early this year as if we would have a Department of Urban Affairs in the federal government, and it may well be the case long before the end of this decade.

The large city and its dwellers have become as American as the denizens of the smaller places. New York and Chicago, along with their inhabitants, are made their homes in such places, about the same as the 16 per cent living in places 500,000 or larger, but much less than the 27.5 per cent living in places over 100,000. About one out of every four *urban* Americans (27 per cent) live in a middle-sized city; Middletown is still as much America as Chicago and New York, even if glamour and sophistication is more concentrated in the larger cities (Table 1).

TABLE 1

NUMBER AND POPULATION OF URBAN PLACES BY TYPE AND SIZE,
AND NUMBER IN RURAL POPULATION, UNITED STATES, 1960

Size of Place	No. of Places	Population (In Millions)	Percentage of Total Population
Urban places:			
1,000,000 or more........	5	17.5	9.8
500,000 to 1,000,000......	16	11.1	6.2
250,000 to 500,000......	30	10.8	6.0
100,000 to 250,000......	81	11.6	6.5
50,000 to 100,000*.....	201	13.8	7.8
25,000 to 50,000*.....	432	14.9	8.3
10,000 to 25,000......	1,134	17.6	9.8
5,000 to 10,000......	1,394	9.8	5.5
2,500 to 5,000......	2,152	7.6	4.2
Other urban territory........	....	10.5	5.8
Rural places.................	....	54.1	30.1
Total...............	....	179.3	100.0

* Middle-sized cities.

now firmly a part of the American scene, having been melted down in the pot along with the others of earlier arriving stock. American Negroes have replaced the immigrants as our metropolitan "problem," but they give thoroughly American flavor to the metropolis.

Although the center of attention has shifted to the metropolis, the middle-sized community is still holding its own. In 1960, there were 633 places in the size range 25,000 to 100,000. Over 16 per cent of the American population

While contemporary social scientists have not produced another Middletown, neither have they been idle. The purpose of this paper is to draw upon some of their work to fill in the gaps between the Lynds' work and the present day. To begin with, we shall attempt to draw a collective portrait of middle-sized cities, drawing heavily on Census materials. As a second topic, it will be worthwhile to review the contents of the Middletown books, an enterprise that will show dramatically the changes which have taken place since that time. Finally we shall take up a topic, interest in which was sparked by the Lynds' second book but which has only recently come into some stature—studies of community politics and social structure. Here we will attempt to characterize how independent cities such as Muncie, Indiana, are "run," a topic that should be of concern to librarians who have to deal with "power structures." We shall also consider very briefly a "new" type of middle-sized city—the suburb, an artifact of population growth surpassing the political boundaries of the metropolitan stars of which they are satellites.

TYPES OF MIDDLE-SIZED CITIES

Of the great metropolitan areas, each has a special flavor of its own concocted of topography, tradition, and the pattern of settlement and replenishment of human stock. Thus, New York is the acknowledged center of fashion, theater, and finance, while Chicago is reputed to be, at best, second to our largest metropolis in almost every respect. These special flavors, however, elude the census counts, for the major metropolitan areas are each so big that they resemble each other in demographic respects more than they differ. To be sure, Detroit has a higher proportion of blue-collar workers than Boston, but both cities resemble each other more than each resembles Ann Arbor. The very size of the major metropolitan areas implies great diversification in getting a living and in the major enterprises dominating the scene.

Not so, however, with middle-sized cities. While each may have its distinctive bouquet, cities of the size range 25,000–100,000 tend to be more individualized and present a greater variety of types than their larger sister cities. Cities of this size tend to specialize, and

this specialization is the source of their diversity. Furthermore, a good proportion of such cities are either contiguous to larger metropolitan areas forming their immediate suburbs or are close enough to be considered satellite communities.

The machinery of the United States Census moves slowly; hence, the best data available on the variety and diversity of American cities dates from the 1950 Census. The data discussed in the next few pages come primarily from Duncan and Reiss's book on the social characteristics of urban and rural places.[2]

One of the most dramatic changes between 1950 and 1960 is the growth in the number of middle-sized cities. In 1950 there were 378 such places and in 1960, 633. In small part this increase is an artifact of changes in the definition of urban places between the two Censuses, but in large part it represents the growth of urban places on the fringes of metropolitan areas. In short, the suburban movement, of which we have heard so much, has increased by more than half the number of independent political entities in the middle-size range. In very practical terms, this increase means a fractionation of municipal services. For example, instead of an increase in the coverage of existing school systems and existing library systems, this has meant the establishment of new systems.

Although there has been a drastic increase in the middle-sized city since 1950, we can expect that the same range of differences will be represented today as in the earlier Census. In 1950, there were some 378 cities in the size range

[2] O. D. Duncan and A. J. Reiss, *Social Characteristics of Urban and Rural Communities, 1950* (New York: John Wiley & Sons, 1956).

25,000 to 100,000. Of these, 98 (or 26 per cent) were the central cities of small standard metropolitan areas; that is to say, they were surrounded by enough other urban places to be classified as a Standard Metropolitan Area (SMA) under the then current Census definition. Another 157 (or 42 per cent) were independent cities not large enough nor

TABLE 2*

CLASSIFICATION OF CITIES OF
25,000 TO 100,000

Type of City	No.	Per Cent
Central Cities:		
50,000 to 100,000......	84	22
Under 50,000..........	14	4
Total Central Cities...	98	26
Suburbs:		
50,000 to 100,000†.....	42	11
25,000 to 50,000......	81	21
Total Suburbs........	123	32
Independent Cities,		
20,000 to 50,000‡......	157	42
Totals§..............	378	100

* Adapted from O. D. Duncan and A. J. Reiss, *Social Characteristics of Urban and Rural Communities, 1950* (New York: John Wiley & Sons, 1956).
† Following the classification system employed by Duncan and Reiss, suburbs include cities contiguous to central cities or within easy commuting distance thereof.
‡ There are no "independent cities" between 50,000 and 100,000, since a city over 50,000 was classified as a central city of a Standard Metropolitan Area in the 1950 Census.
§ Unincorporated places, regardless of size, are not included in this tabulation.

surrounded by enough urbanized places to qualify as an SMA. The remaining 123 (or 32 per cent) were suburbs or satellites of larger urban places (Table 2). Incidentally, Muncie, Indiana, qualifies as the central city of an SMA of some 90,000 in 1950, even though its population was then 58,000, barely qualifying it for consideration as an SMA.

Suburbs and satellites tend to be more concentrated in the northeastern sector of the country, while the smaller SMA's and independent cities are more characteristically found in the more sparsely settled areas of the South and Southwest.

Suburbs and satellite cities generally fall into one of two major types. On the one hand, there are the dormitory suburbs, with some local industry but primarily engaged in housing and feeding those who are employed elsewhere, as, for example, Hempstead, New York, or Highland Park, Illinois. Then there are the industrial satellites dependent on the central city for wholesale trade functions but employing a large proportion of its labor force in manufacturing, as Linden, New Jersey, or Gary, Indiana.

Independent cities or the smaller central cities of SMA's tend either to be manufacturing centers in their own rights, as, for example, Zanesville, Ohio, or Muncie, Indiana; or they are trading centers for a hinterland, such as Fresno, California, or Asheville, North Carolina.

I should emphasize that there are few cities in this size class which are completely devoid of industry or which carry on absolutely no wholesale or retail trade. The classification of a city depends more on where it stands on a continuum rather than in a discrete class. Furthermore, to these types must be added other classifications: Some cities serve as important educational centers, such as Madison, Wisconsin, and Ann Arbor, Michigan, even though they are also manufacturing centers and trading centers. Others provide important recreational functions—for example, Atlantic City, New Jersey, or Asheville, North Carolina.

Corresponding to its functional classification, a city varies in its demographic composition. Non-manufacturing suburbs have populations with higher levels of educational attainment and a larger proportion of their working force in the white-collar occupations. Not surprisingly, suburban cities have higher incomes and a higher proportion of persons owning their own homes. Manufacturing suburbs have lower educational levels than dormitory suburbs but higher educational levels than independent cities, higher incomes and—surprisingly—lower levels of home ownership.

In short, the middle-sized city is not a homogeneous category, but it rather includes a diversity of urban places of which particular characteristics vary in types of economic bases and corresponding demographic compositions.

To capture the flavor of life as lived in the middle-sized city, our Census data are of little use. For this information we must turn to the sociological monograph. What better place to start than with a review of the classic Lynd studies?

LOOKING BACKWARD AT MIDDLETOWN

No matter how skilfully portrayed by the Lynds, Middletown in the twenties and thirties could never represent the whole of America at those periods. It was (and still is) an "independent" city, not tied closely into a great metropolitan complex. Middetowners were primarily native born of native-born stock. And, perhaps most important, Middletown in its cultural aspects represented, if anything, the northeastern industrialized sector of our country.

To today's reader it is an unfamiliar scene that the Lynds painted in the twenties and thirties. In the earlier period, Middletown was just beginning to enter the automobile and radio ages.

Middletowners in the working class still worked a sixty-hour week, rising at 5 A.M. and working a full shift on Saturday. The Ball Mason jar factories closed down for a full month in the summer time because of the intense heat of the furnaces. Business-class Middletowners worked shorter hours, but still longer than their counterparts today. Some of the clerical employees worked only a half-day on Saturday, but the five-day week was not in effect.

A good proportion of Middletown streets were still unpaved and many homes were yet to be connected to the city sewer system. An automobile trip as far as Toledo was a grand adventure, and goods and people moved into and out of Muncie primarily by rail. Typhoid took its toll every summer; only a minority of Middletowners were born in hospitals.

Most striking is the almost complete absence of the welfare state. Muncie's industrial plants hired and fired their workers frequently, reacting quickly to changes in inventory and sales. There was no minimum wage and only a minimum of labor organization. Unemployment compensation, old-age pensions, and public assistance were yet to be adopted. Their absence made life on the working-cass level of Muncie capricious and arbitrary. Along with the absence of welfare-state institutions went a set of cultural values that meant a "no frills" city government and educational system. Middletowners used their public library, but their public library was not regarded as an important institution by city fathers and the business elite that ran the town.

In the thirties, one could hear the soft padding of the feet on which "socialism" crept into American life. The welfare legislation of the New Deal had begun, and the city government was beginning to expand its service and welfare functions. Middletown rearranged itself politically in the thirties, with the business class aligned against the working class. Unions were being organized. Education was being extended into the policy of a high-school education for all, and even the library established new branches to serve the working-class areas of the town.

Thirty and forty years ago the control of the community was still in the hands of the business class with local industrialists playing a major role. In their second volume, the Lynds devoted an entire chapter to the "X" family, showing how, through the ownership and control of the community's important institutions, this family's influence was felt in almost every sphere of life in Middletown. Locally owned industry still played a major role in the city's economic life, although in the thirties the ancillary manufacturing plants of major automobile companies were beginning to gain more and more importance. Middletown was becoming a place where branch factories of large corporations were established.

Much has happened to America since the Lynds pedaled their bicycles around Muncie and interviewed the natives. The material position of the American population has advanced tremendously. Automobile ownership, once a wistfully desired status among Middletowners, has now diffused so widely that more land is dedicated to storing and moving the automobile than to any other activity. A host of other material inventions has improved the comfort of the American population.

Most striking have been the changes in the conception of the role of the state in cushioning the trauma of vital processes and shifts in the economy. Educational activities typically absorb close to half of tax revenues expended at the local level, with welfare (particularly old-age assistance) accounting for another major portion. Through the efforts of private philanthropy and public support, all but a few babies are now born in hospitals, and typhoid is now a rare disease rather than a recurrent summer epidemic. The welfare state, in short, is here.

All this has been accompanied and is partially generated by radical changes in technology and the social organization of the American economy. The "Middletowns" of America have been affected radically by these changes. Even though we may not know the details of what has occurred in Muncie, we know that the flavor of life in the class of which Muncie is a member has been altered. The changes I want to stress in the next section of this paper are those that have drastically affected the control system of American communities, particularly those that, like Middletown, are not suburban satellites.

THE "X" FAMILY REVISITED

When the Lynds made their second visit to Muncie, they were struck by a characteristic of the town that was not salient to them in the twenties. Because the "X" family enterprise had weathered the depression very well, the "X's" had consolidated and increased their strength in the community. In almost every sphere of Middletown life, the "X" family had some measure of potential control. Furthermore, the managers of the absentee-owned factories—GM and Delco-Remy—played little direct role in Middletown affairs except to exercise a firm veto (using the threat to leave) when and if local labor looked obstreperous enough to organize.

Much has changed in the Middletowns of the 1950's. There are few "X" families left, and the managers of the absentee-owned factories are playing a different sort of role today from that they acted in the past. Indeed, dramatic changes have also taken place in Muncie itself. A few months ago, the Ball Mason Jar Company announced that it was removing its plant from Muncie to a southern location. Newspaper reports at the time reported Muncie's mayor as stating that the loss was not too great because the city's industry is now very diversified! The Ball family (known as the "X" family in the Lynds' book) has literally left Muncie, just as their counterparts have declined in numbers in other communities throughout the land.

To understand the implications of the change in the pattern control and ownership of industrial and commercial enterprises for the political and administrative systems of local communities, we have to step back for a moment and take an even longer historical perspective than is provided by the Lynds' work. The trend toward large-scale industrial enterprises is a long-term one, and we have to go back to the nineteenth century to find a period when the control and ownership of industrial and commercial enterprises was in the hands of the local population of the middle-sized city.

In the nineteenth-century middle-sized American community, there was a more unified fabric of community life. If a man was a successful industrialist or a successful professional man, he tended also to be recognized as a community leader in a wide variety of local

institutions, lodges and churches, for example, but most important, in public office. Several research studies (notably Dahl's,[3] Schulze's,[4] and my own[5]) have found that the participation of industrial and commercial leaders in political life was much more frequent in this earlier period than at present. In part, this was because the working class had yet to organize itself politically to challenge the hegemony of the business class. Furthermore, the major community-wide institution was local government, while today there are many other institutions which compete with local government as guardians of the local commonweal.

Indeed, when we compare the contemporary community with the nineteenth-century counterpart, the most striking characteristic of the former is the relative drop in the importance accorded to local government not only in comparison with the state and federal government but also in relation to the importance accorded to local voluntary associations. This appears to be the age of the "community project" in which significant community enterprises are often initiated outside the framework of local government, aided and abetted by a proliferation of civic associations and citizen committees. In many communities, we see the mayor and the city council apparently dragging their heels while civic associations and citizen committees exhort the community to move toward Progress.

[3] Robert A. Dahl, *Who Governs?* (New Haven: Yale University Press, 1961).

[4] Robert O. Schulze, "The Bifurcation of Power in a Satellite City," in M. Janowitz (ed.), *Community Political Systems* (New York: Free Press of Glencoe, 1961).

[5] P. H. Rossi and R. A. Dentler, *The Politics of Urban Renewal: The Chicago Findings* (New York: Free Press of Glencoe, 1961).

Parenthetically, it should be noted that the Lynds paid a great deal of attention to the voluntary associations in Middletown of the time but were not particularly impressed with the devotion of the associations to the commonweal. I think the descriptive phrases would have to be changed were the Lynds to study another Middletown today.

Another striking characteristic of the American community is the status gap between the personnel of local government and the local elites of wealth and status. The local echelons of the party organizations and the elective offices of municipal and county government are manned by persons whose social positions and attainments are often several levels below those of the denizens of the country club, Rotary, and the Chamber of Commerce. Money, status, and intellect seem to cluster in one place and political control in another.

What has happened to bring this about? The main source of the imbalance appears to be the lack of correspondence between the way in which our economy is organized as compared with our lowest level of government.

There are literally millions of business enterprises in this country, yet all but a very small percentage employ a minority of our labor force. For example, one out of every ten workers is employed either by one or the other of our two leading business enterprises—General Motors and American Telephone and Telegraph. It is a rare community in which the major employers are locally owned and operated companies. The industrial managers who are in command on the local scene tend to be itinerants serving out their duty time in "Middletown."

Local government, in contrast, is locally defined and controlled. An aspirant to local office is nominated by his coresidents, and, if successful, is elected by a majority of the local electorate. Success in local politics is based, therefore, on being well known.

Merton had distinguished between "local" and "cosmopolitan" leaders in his study[6] of Dover, New Jersey. Locals are those whose leadership position is based on being at the center of a widespread network of personal acquaintanceship leading to political office-holding, while cosmopolitan leaders are those whose position is based on the holding of some expertise or the control of significant amounts of resources. Locals run the political machinery of the local community, while cosmopolitans tend to run the service clubs and civic associations. Note that the latter positions are not subject to mass control, but, even when elected, cosmopolitans are put into office by small minorities of the local population.

While what I have described above is built around the social structure of an industrial community, the same sort of bifurcation occurs in the dormitory suburb. The "locals" in such a suburb tend to be recruited from the same sources, small business and the minor professions (law and real estate), whose clientele are local residents and whose roots in the community are considerable. The downtown manager and professional who spends his nights in the suburbs is at a disadvantage both in mustering enough time away from the demands of his downtown job and in

[6] R. K. Merton, "Patterns of Influence: Local and Cosmopolitan Influentials" in *Social Theory and Social Structure* (Glencoe, Ill.: Free Press, 1957).

building up the level of personal acquaintanceship necessary to make it possible for him to successfully run for office. The tensions between the "natives" and the "exurbanites" in some communities have been sufficient to break out in the form of community conflicts over fluoridation, the schools, and even the library catalog.

It may be easier for the cosmopolitan to penetrate areas of community political life other than the city council. School boards and library boards, particularly, have had their share of cosmopolitans, where their greater educational and occupational accomplishments seem to carry weight with the electorate. It should also be pointed out that this pattern of recruitment is a tribute to school superintendents and librarians who have managed to achieve a public definition of their boards as "different" from other political offices.

The lack of congruence between the control over the economic base of a community and its political definition has led in many middle-sized cities to an ambiguity in the location of power. In Middletown in the thirties, the Lynds saw everything leading back to the "X" family and its business-class allies. With the end of locally owned large-scale industrial enterprises and the rising independent political power of the working class, we have begun to note a double-headed pyramid of power.

On the one hand, the machinery of local government, whether operated under Democratic or Republican labels, is firmly in the hands of the locals. Here is the camping ground of the small downtown lawyer, merchant, or real estate broker. The political life of these communities is sensitive to the demands of solidary groups, such as labor unions, neighborhood associations, veterans' associations, and the like, which because of their large membership are reputed to be able to muster public opinion on one or another side of potential issues.

On the other hand, the machinery of local civic associations tends to be in the hands of the industrial cosmopolitans who, because they can command resources, tend to dominate. I have in mind particularly the local chambers of commerce, Community Chests, Welfare Councils, and the like. Library and school boards tend to be run more like the Welfare Council than like the City Council. Within the voluntary community associations, which depend so largely on the bounty of large contributors, wealth and its control can and does play a major part.

This pattern of separation of control over central community institutions appears to be particularly strong where industrial workers and the business and professional class are in opposite political camps. For this reason, middle-sized industrial cities of the Northeast are more likely to show this separation of control than their sister cities in the South.

One important consequence of this pattern of control is the very different contemporary status of labor unions on the local scene. When the Lynds studied Muncie in the thirties, labor organizations were still politically unsavory and the Lynds describe an incident in which the local General Motors plant managers paid for the augmentation of the police force in anticipation of "labor trouble." Today, the local police are either neutral or slightly on the side of labor. Indeed, in some cities like Gary, Indiana, local government can scarcely be regarded as neutral, and even the local merchants advertise unlimited credit available to strikers for the duration.

Another important consequence, especially for this particular audience, is the augmented stature of such professional positions as school superintendent, public health officer, and librarian. The competition between the public and private sectors of the local community, each vying with the other as champions of the commonweal, has given the community professionals a better opportunity to increase and augment the services that they provide. For example, in one community I have studied, the librarian has been able to define the library as the special concern of the business elite, obtaining funds and capital expenditures for the library almost out of proportion to what the community needs. In other communities, perceptive and energetic school superintendents have played the same game to the benefit of the school system. There are dangers as well as benefits to be derived, however. All too often the library, hospital, or school system can become the battleground over which "locals" and "cosmopolitans" struggle.

It is significant to note that because the "cosmopolitans" appear to have the sorts of talents that are recognized by promotions and advancement within the large corporation, this does not mean that they have a monopoly on *all talents*. The locals who run the political apparatus of city government often have considerable talents that are important in the running of the collective enterprise of the community. A successful politician is one who goes through a long series of negotiations, compromises, and trading. The talents that go into managing an industrial enterprise are not those that are needed in forging consensus in a local community. Command is not so important or critical as the art of ascertaining consensus and building it out of diversity. Reformist political officials, intent on building a rational public policy, often fail to see that policies, to be effective, need to be supported as well as to be rational. The local, because of his sensitivity to the local community and because of his ability to lead public opinion, is more suited to the role of community public leader than the cosmopolitan. There are different orders of skills involved in the roles taken by these two types, each of which complements the other. The fortunate community is one in which the locals and the cosmopolitans recognize that they are mutually complementary and have actively worked out a division of labor.

CONCLUSION

The task of bringing the Lynds' classics up to date is obviously too great for the kind of brief overview that a paper of this length can provide. Much more has transpired in the generation since their last book than could be mentioned here. We have tried instead to look at one area of community life in some depth, using the perspective provided by their work.

We have also tried to give a brief view of the diversity among middle-sized cities in America. There is no Middletown any longer, and indeed there probably never was, but rather a variety of middle-sized cities varying according to their economic bases, their demographic compositions, and their dependence on the major metropolitan areas.

The major portion of this paper has been devoted to summarizing recent studies of community power structures in America. Studies of power have proliferated in the past decade precisely because power has been so difficult to locate on the local level. The geographic basis of political power in this country has not kept pace with the development of industrial enterprises. The employment of the majority of our population is in business enterprises that are regional and national in character, but our political life is still defined locally. This has meant that the hegemony of industrialism and industrialists can be counterbalanced on the local political scene. The democratic nature of our society has benefited in the sense that there is apparently more access to power than was formerly the case. But at the same time, the parochial interests of particular localities have been given more weight than might be ideal from the viewpoint of a more tightly organized society.

There are lessons to be learned in this development for the practicing professional on the local level. Because the locus of power is shifting and ephemeral, how to get things done seems more and more problematical. But for the clever and gifted practitioner this same ambiguity means that there are many more levers to be pulled to achieve his professional ends.

FINANCIAL SUPPORT OF LOCAL GOVERNMENTAL SERVICES
WITH SPECIAL REFERENCE TO PUBLIC LIBRARIES
IN CITIES OF MEDIUM SIZE

SIMEON E. LELAND

THE topic of financial support of local governmental services is one of the most important in public finance. It represents a complex of problems; many are difficult of solution.

Not long ago the local units were spending more money than the federal government. Their direct tax burdens rested more heavily on citizens than the taxes of the national government. This condition may be pleasant to remember. Today (1960) the federal government spends over $97 billion annually while state and local governments together spend over $70 billion, with local governments spending $7.3 billion more than the states.[1]

The 675 cities with more than 25,000 inhabitants in 1960 contained over 76,000,000 inhabitants out of an urban population of 116,000,000.[2] The 17,368 places with less than 25,000 inhabitants accounted for less than 40,000,000 people. The "middle-sized" cities, which are the concern of this conference, range from 25,000 or 35,000 to 100,000 inhabitants.[3]

In 1960 there were 545 cities with population groups from 25,000 to 100,000. They accounted for over 25,000,000 people in the aggregate. Their total revenues were $2,690 million out of $15,251 million for all 18,043 cities in the United States.[4] Although there are 545 cities in the population size group of 25,000 to 100,000, there are 886 public libraries serving population areas of this size. These libraries are 11.8 per cent of the nation's public libraries.[5] This fact would seem to indicate that the public library is more of a community service than an urban phenomenon. On the other hand, 70.9 per cent of the employees of local libraries are hired by municipalities, 17.2 per cent work for counties, 7.7 per cent for special districts, and 4.2 per cent for townships.[6] But inasmuch as national data on library finances are almost wholly lacking (there being no revenue information beyond income aggregates and some classified expenditures dealing primarily with salaries and book purchases), it is essen-

---

[1] Total governmental expenditures, 1960, excluding duplicate transactions between levels of government, were as follows (in millions of dollars):

Federal	$97,284
State	31,596
Local	38,895

See *Governmental Finances in 1960* (Department of Commerce, Bureau of the Census, G-GF60, No. 2 [September 19, 1961]), p. 16.

[2] *City Government Finances in 1960* (Department of Commerce, Bureau of the Census, G-CF60, No. 2), p. 1.

[3] The Census Bureau in its financial statistics of cities breaks its size classification at 25,000 in some years and 30,000 in other years, while the *Library Statistics* of the United States Department of Health, Education, and Welfare begin at 35,000.

[4] *City Government Finances in 1960*, pp. 1, 8.

[5] *Library Statistics* (Department of Health, Education and Welfare, Office of Education, OE-15034 [March 1962]), p. 4.

[6] *1957 Census of Governments, Compendium of Public Employment*, II, No. 2 (Washington, D.C.: Department of Commerce, Bureau of the Census, August, 1958), 17.

tial to approach their revenue problems through information available generally on municipal and "local" finances. Many of the libraries are in fact branches of the city governments in which they operate. Some are administered, it is believed, as other departments within the particular local government structures. Some are under the direct administrative control of local library boards—presumably non-partisan and independent of the city government itself—but depend upon such governments for tax levies or appropriations of funds. Still others are part of local school systems, or depend on school authorities to levy taxes or make appropriations. No matter what the precise arrangements, the libraries in our cities are part and parcel of the local government structure and share in their fiscal problems. Eight states seem to have made provision for independent special library districts[7] (Table 1).

[7] The *1957 Census of Governments* indicates that there are 322 special library districts out of a total of 14,405 special districts in the United States (I, No. 1 [September 1957], 7).

TABLE 1

SPECIAL LIBRARY DISTRICTS IN LOCAL GOVERNMENTS, 1957

State	No. of Districts	How Organized	Financial Powers
California.......	7	Created by county board of supervisors on petition of electors	Levy taxes; issue bonds; accept gifts
Delaware........	*	Established by boards of education	Supported by school district tax levies
Idaho..........	2	Established by county boards of commissioners	Levy taxes; issue bonds
Illinois..........	12	Established by county judge	Levy property taxes
Indiana.........	215	⎰1901 law—establishment by city or town 1917 law—establishment by county commissioners 1947 law—formed by resolution of governing body of any municipal corporation on petition of voters⎱	Levy taxes; issue bonds
Iowa...........	1	County library districts, composed of one or more adjacent counties—established by County Board of Supervisors	Levy property tax
Kansas.........	2*	Regional library boards	....
Maryland.......	*	County library boards	....
Michigan........	*	County library boards	....
Missouri........	36	County library districts established by County Courts	Amount of taxes to be levied determined by electors
Nevada.........	*	County library boards	....
New Hampshire..	*	Township public library districts	....
Ohio............	32	County library districts created by county commissioners; regional library districts (two or more counties) created by joint resolution of county commissioners. (Other governments permitted to administer libraries.)	Determine amount of tax levies; accept gifts
South Carolina...	*	County public libraries created by special acts of legislature	....
Washington.....	15	Rural library districts created by county commissioners; intercounty rural library districts created by two or more county boards of commissioners at joint session. School boards also can create public libraries and levy taxes or make appropriations for support.	....
West Virginia....	*	County library boards	....

* Not counted as a separate local governmental unit by Bureau of the Census.

Source: Compiled from *1957 Census of Governments, Local Government Structur*, Vol. I, No. 3 (January, 1958). For number districts on each state, see *ibid.*, No. 1 (September, 1957), 31.

LIBRARY EXPENDITURES

From the standpoint of cost, libraries are a relatively minor—I shall not say, "unimportant"—activity of city governments. Out of over $15,250 million spent by city governments in 1960, the public libraries accounted for only $185 million (Table 2). This was only 1.2 per cent of the total. Only water transport and terminals, general public buildings, and liquor store expenditures were credited with smaller amounts. Utility expenditures—for water, electricity, etc., including operations, capital outlays, and interest on debt—were the largest item of expenditures and accounted for 19 per cent of the total. Education ranked next with about 12 per cent of the total and then highways with 10.3 per cent.

Since library expenditures represented so small an amount—both relatively and absolutely—in the total of city expenditures it might be supposed that they might be neglected and that over time the actual position of the public library among the many other functions of government might be worsened. Education, police, fire protection, public health, sanitation, and similar functions have traditionally been activities of major importance to cities. New functions,

TABLE 2

FUNCTIONAL DISTRIBUTION OF EXPENDITURES OF CITY GOVERNMENTS, 1930–60

FUNCTION	EXPENDITURES (MILLIONS)		PER CENT OF TOTAL		PER CENT INCREASE OVER 1930
	1960	1930	1960	1930	
Police	$ 1,275	$ 243	8.4	6.4	425
Fire	885	186	5.8	4.9	376
Other public safety	....	42	....	1.1	....
Highways	1,573	605	10.3	15.9	160
Sanitation	1,332	277	8.7	7.3	381
Public welfare	608	80*	4.0	2.1	660
Education	1,801	999†	11.8	26.2	80
LIBRARIES	185	38	1.2	1.0	387
Health and hospitals	799	143	5.2	3.7	459
Parks and recreation	551	114	3.6	3.0	383
Housing and community development	464	....	3.0	....	....
Water transport and terminals	63	....	0.4	....	....
Airports	189	....	1.2	....	....
General control (general government, 1930)	598	205	3.9	5.4	192
General public buildings	182	....	1.2	....	....
Interest on general debt	431	407†	2.8	10.7	6
Other and unallocable	883	40§	5.8	1.0	2,108
Utility expenditures	2,915	405‖	19.1	10.6	620
Liquor stores expenditure	60	....	0.4	....	....
Insurance trust expenditure	458	....	3.0	....	....
Correction	....	26	0.2	0.7	....
Total	$15,252	$3,810	100.0	100.0	300

* Includes charities, supervision, care of poor, care of children, other charities, and aid to special classes, such as soldiers, sailors, and mothers.

† Includes schools, recreational expenditures classified as "educational," and pensions in regard to schools.

‡ Includes payments for interest on funded and floating debt, special assessment debt and other debts, and administration of public trust fund investments.

§ Includes pensions not included above, judgments and losses, unclassified and undistributed, and miscellaneous outlays.

‖ Includes outlays.

Source: Compiled from *Financial Statistics of Cities Having a Population of Over 30,000: 1930* (Department of Commerce, Bureau of the Census); *Compendium of City Government Finances in 1960* (Department of Commerce, Bureau of the Census).

such as public welfare, housing, and airports, have also been added in the last generation. Nevertheless, if comparison is made between functional expenditures in 1960 and 1930, the position of the public library has slightly improved[8] (Table 2). The actual dollars spent on libraries increased from $38 to $185 million in this thirty-year period—an increase of 387 per cent. Police expenditures increased 425 per cent, fire prevention 376 per cent, health and hospitals 459 per cent, parks and recreation 363 per cent. Expenditures for education, on the other hand, rose 80 per cent and highways only twice as much—not indicating any tapering off of interest in either of these fields, but probably because of the fact that in each case very large numbers are involved and substantial increases in amounts at these expenditure levels do not produce correspondingly large percentage increases. The amounts spent on libraries may not be adequate either according to desired standards of library service or in accord with citizen desires, whatever they may be, but it is significant that over the last generation the financial position of public libraries, measured by volume of expenditures, has improved. The difficulty of getting adequate statistics on this subject by no

[8] Attention must be called to the fact that the functional tabulations of expenditures by the Census Bureau were not identical for these years, but the author attempted some reclassifications to facilitate comparison. The footnotes to Table 2 attempt to show the inclusions for 1930 groupings. It is believed that in spite of some inevitable mistakes in regrouping data general trends can be discerned. The functional classification of expenditures of local governments made by the 1957 Census of Governments and covering the period from 1902 to 1957 unfortunately does not consider libraries in its classification. (see *1957 Census of Governments, Historical Summary of Governmental Finances in the United States*, IV, No. 3 [June, 1959], 22–23).

means indicates a decline in public support—nor does it indicate that library expenditures are what they should be.

PRESSURE FOR EXPENDITURES

One of the problems confronting all of those interested in small, or minor, activities of government—and again no invidious distinction is meant—is that the pressure for funds being what it is, appropriations tend to grow most where greatest pressures for increases are exerted. The suppression of crime, the alleviation of economic hardships for the unemployed, the care of the aged, the orphaned, and the sick, the education of the young, as well as provision for streets and highways—all expenditures calling for large sums of money and all reinforced by active pressure groups—combine to increase the difficulties of getting appropriations from various legislative bodies for the other or "neglected" functions. This state of affairs affects not only libraries but also the support of art museums, symphony orchestras, operas, institutions of higher education, and other cultural activities. Their importance is increasing not only as a phase of our social evolution but as a part of the education of our society. Some of these institutions—of a public character and not as philanthropic organizations—have been so divorced from general government and from our educational system that they are not always regarded as essential parts of either. With administrative separation, largely to insure independence from partisan politics, has gone financial divorcement and the inadequate support of these important cultural activities. This generalization may be challenged, but, unfortunately, we do not have the data to determine whether libraries, for example, are more adequately supported: (1) if they are separate political bodies, (2) if they are a department of a given local government, (3) if they are operated as part of the school system (with or without independent boards), or (4) if they are organized in some other way. The important thing is that in the last generation public libraries have not lost in their financial support, nor in public esteem, nor in their contributions to society.

DEPRECIATION OF MONEY

In spite of what has been said about increases in the demand and standards for public services over the last thirty years, it must not be assumed that this is the sole explanation for increases in the volume or level of public expenditures. Increases in cost and depreciation in the value of money over time have played a conspicuous part in increasing the aggregates. Not all public services have been affected equally. There is no point, however, for purposes of this paper in reducing the data to terms of constant dollars. The focus here is rather upon the revenue side of the problem. Here, too, the problem has been aggravated by the shrinkage in the value of the dollar, necessitating the raising of even larger amounts of revenue to cover the cost of given units of service. For individual taxpayers the inflationary increases in income have increased the sharpness of taxes imposed at progressive rates. Even property taxes and capital gains taxes have been increased as valuations have reflected declines in the value of money. Thus, no small part of the tax increases over the lives of many citizens have been due to dollar shrinkages. And no small part of the problems of local finances also centers here.

SOURCES OF REVENUE

The sources of revenue utilized by local governments can be understood most clearly if a brief historical survey is made of the taxes imposed by the various levels of government. Such a survey will indicate the trends that have developed, as well as current sources of funds. The *1957 Census of Governments* has made it possible to present these comparisons beginning with 1902.

FEDERAL REVENUES

No taxpayer needs to be reminded that the most important source of federal funds is the personal income tax and its counterpart, the corporate income tax. These are the most productive taxes utilized by any political unit in the United States. They account for the ability of the federal government to finance wars, to hold its dominant place in world affairs, and to help support a vast range of activities carried on by the state and local units. Two important facts contribute to the dominance of these taxes in the federal system: (1) the income taxes are centrally administered by the national government itself —there is no division or sharing of authority for enforcement or collection with other governmental units.[9] (2) The total income of citizens and the product of our national economic and commercial life are within its reach. There are no state or local boundary lines to defeat its jurisdiction or to place tax-paying capacity beyond its reach. So productive is the federal system that there is reason to believe that estimated revenue yields are more important in determining expenditures than the reverse,

[9] The federal estate tax is an exception. Both state and local units participate in the administration of death taxes.

as in the case with local units, where the estimated cost of activities to be undertaken fixes the amounts and levels of taxation to be imposed. The stability of all centrally administered tax rates tends to create this condition.

The details of federal revenues are shown in Table 3. The historic shift from indirect to direct taxation is also quite clear. Before World War I customs duties plus excises on alcoholic beverages and tobacco products produced from 63 to 73 per cent of federal revenues. In 1960, the federal income tax on persons and corporations accounted for about 62 per cent of total national revenues. Indirect taxes in 1960 produced only about 12.5 per cent of total federal funds.[10]

STATE REVENUES

A long-term survey of state revenues reveals four major developments:

1. The decline in the importance of the general property tax
2. The rise of centrally administered state taxes
3. The increasing importance of funds received from the federal government for the support of some state functions and their subsequent transfer by the state to local units
4. The advent of motor vehicle taxes and liquor revenues

These developments are shown in Table 4.

The decline in the property tax and the growth of centrally administered state taxes are about like the two sides of a coin. The property tax does not lend itself to local administration. It was realized, too, that if the states were to have highly productive—as well as fairly equitable—taxes the states would have to administer them. Dependence

[10] Based upon yield of customs duties, motor fuel, alcoholic beverage, tobacco products, and other sales and gross-receipts taxes.

on local machinery was inefficient, costly, and productive of many injustices. Centrally administered property taxes on railroads, public utilities, and corporations were followed by state-administered corporation, income, sales, motor fuel, and other taxes. In 1960 the most important sources of state revenue were sales and gross-receipts taxes (32.0 per cent of total) and intergovernmental revenues (20.5 per cent of total). In 1902 there were no state personal or corporate income taxes, no motor fuel taxes or vehicle licenses; even liquor store revenues were negligible. The evolution of the state revenue system is clearly discernible from Table 4.

LOCAL REVENUES

The historical survey of local revenues is based on data from counties, cities, townships, school districts, and a wide variety of special districts characteristic of local government throughout the United States. Table 5 covers statistics from 102,279 local governments for 1957. Of the number, school districts constituted almost half of the total. Cities accounted for the bulk of revenues and expenditures. Townships were fiscally of least importance, though there was little difference between total number of cities and number of counties.

Even though the historical survey of local finances includes other units, this paper is primarily concerned with the problems of middle-sized cities. Nevertheless, it is believed that the important trends can be clearly seen from a tabulation that covers all local units. Moreover, such a table provides completeness of coverage and makes it possible to compare revenues of the levels of government. Not to be overlooked either is the fact that libraries are oper-

TABLE 3

FEDERAL REVENUES, 1902–60

Sources of Revenue	1960	1957	1952	1942	1932	1922	1913	1902
	Amount (Millions)							
Total............................	$100,739	$87,066	$71,798	$16,062	$2,634	$4,261	$962	$653
General revenue..................	88,027	78,403	66,615	14,788	2,542	4,221	962	653
Taxes.........................	77,003	69,815	59,744	12,265	1,813	3,371	662	513
Individual income.............	40,715	35,620	27,921	3,205	405	1,939	35	......
Corporation income...........	21,494	21,167	21,226	4,727	598			......
Sales, gross receipts, and customs	12,603	11,127	9,332	3,425	733	1,152	612	487
Customs duties.............	1,105	735	532	369	311	318	310	243
Motor fuel................	1,984	1,498	720	370	......	......	......	......
Alcoholic beverages.........	3,106	2,893	2,549	1,037	8	44	223	187
Tobacco products...........	1,927	1,669	1,565	779	398	270	77	49
Other sales and gross-receipt taxes.................	4,481	4,333	3,966	870	16	520	2	8
Death and gift...............	1,606	1,365	818	421	41	139	......	5
Other taxes.................	585	537	446	487	36	142	15	21
Charges and miscellaneous general revenue......................	11,024	8,588	6,871	2,523	730	850	300	140
Postal receipts...............	......	2,512	1,967	860	588	485	267	122
Sales of agricultural products...	......	2,092	800	385	......	......	......	......
Other charges and miscellaneous general revenue.............	......	3,984	4,104	1,278	142	365	33	18
Insurance trust revenue...........	12,712	8,663	5,183	1,274	91	40	......	......
	Per Cent of Total							
Total............................	100.00	100.00	100.00	100.00	100.00	100.00	100.00	100.00
General revenue..................	87.4	90.1	92.8	92.1	96.5	99.1	100.0	100.0
Taxes.........................	76.4	80.2	83.2	76.4	68.8	79.1	68.8	78.6
Individual income.............	40.4	40.9	38.9	20.0	15.4	45.5	......	......
Corporation income...........	21.3	24.3	29.6	29.4	22.7		3.6	......
Sales, gross receipts, and customs	12.5	12.8	13.0	21.3	27.8	27.0	63.6	74.6
Customs duties.............	1.1	.8	.7	2.3	11.8	7.5	32.2	37.2
Motor fuel................	2.0	1.7	1.0	2.3	......	......	......	......
Alcoholic beverages.........	3.1	3.3	3.6	6.5	.3	1.0	23.2	28.6
Tobacco products...........	1.9	1.9	2.2	4.8	15.1	6.3	8.0	7.5
Other sales and gross-receipt taxes.................	4.4	5.0	5.5	5.4	.6	12.2	.2	1.2
Death and gift...............	1.6	1.6	1.1	2.6	1.5	3.3	......	.8
Other taxes.................	.6	.6	.6	3.0	1.4	3.3	1.6	3.2
Charges and miscellaneous general revenue......................	11.0	9.9	9.6	15.7	27.7	19.9	31.2	21.4
Postal receipts...............	......	2.9	2.7	5.3	22.3	11.4	27.8	18.7
Sales of agricultural products...	......	2.4	1.1	2.4	......	......	......	......
Other charges and miscellaneous general revenue.............	......	4.6	5.7	8.0	5.4	8.5	3.4	2.7
Insurance trust revenue...........	12.6	9.9	7.2	7.9	3.5	.9	......	......

Source: *Summary of Governmental Finances in 1960* (Department of Commerce, Bureau of the Census, G-GF60, No. 1 [August 18, 1961]); *1957 Census of Governments, Historical Summary of Governmental Finances in the United States*, IV, No. 3.

TABLE 4

STATE REVENUES, 1902–60

Sources of Revenue	1960	1957	1952	1942	1932	1922	1913	1902
	Amount (Millions)							
Total..........................	$32,838	$24,656	$16,815	$ 6,870	$ 2,541	$ 1,360	$376	$192
Total general revenue (direct and intergovernmental).............	27,363	20,382	13,429	5,132	2,423	1,254	376	190
Intergovernmental revenue:								
From federal government.........	6,382	3,500	2,329	802	222	99	6	3
From local governments..........	363	427	156	56	45	27	10	6
Revenue from state sources........	26,093	20,728	14,330	6,012	2,274	1,234	360	183
General revenue from state sources.	20,618	16,454	10,944	4,274	2,156	1,128	360	181
Taxes.......................	18,036	14,531	9,857	3,903	1,890	947	301	156
Individual income............	2,209	1,563	913	249	74	43	....	....
Corporation income..........	1,180	984	838	269	79	58	....	....
Sales and gross receipts.......	10,510	8,436	5,730	2,218	726	134	55	28
General....................	4,302	3,373	2,229	632	7	....	....	....
Motor fuel.................	3,335	2,828	1,870	940	527	13	....	....
Alcoholic beverages........	650	569	442	257	....	....	2	....
Tobacco products..........	923	556	449	130	19	....	....	....
Public utilities.............	365	....	....	....	....	....	....	....
Other sales and gross-receipts taxes...................	935	1,109	740	258	173	121	53	28
Property....................	607	479	370	264	328	348	140	82
Motor vehicle and operators' licenses....................	1,573	1,368	924	431	335	152	5	....
Other taxes.................	1,955	1,701	1,082	472	348	212	101	46
Charges and miscellaneous general revenue........................	2,583	1,923	1,087	370	266	181	59	25
Liquor stores revenue...............	1,128	1,065	924	373	....	....	....	2
Insurance trust revenue.............	4,347	3,209	2,462	1,366	118	106	....	....
	Per Cent of Total							
Total..........................	100.0	100.0	100.0	100.0	100.0	100.0	100.0	100.0
Total general revenue (direct and intergovernmental)...............	83.3	82.7	79.9	74.7	95.4	92.2	100.0	99.0
Intergovernmental revenue:								
From federal government.........	19.4	14.2	13.9	11.7	8.7	7.3	1.6	1.6
From local governments..........	1.1	1.7	.9	.8	1.8	2.0	2.7	3.1
Revenue from state sources.........	79.5	84.0	85.2	87.5	89.5	90.7	95.7	95.3
General revenue from state sources.	62.8	66.7	65.1	62.2	84.8	82.9	95.7	94.3
Taxes.......................	54.9	58.9	58.6	56.8	74.4	69.6	80.0	81.3
Individual income............	6.7	6.3	5.4	3.6	2.9	3.1	....	....
Corporation income..........	3.6	4.0	5.0	3.9	3.1	4.3	....	....
Sales and gross receipts.......	32.0	34.2	34.1	32.3	28.6	9.8	14.6	14.6
General....................	13.1	13.7	13.3	9.2	.3	....	....	....
Motor fuel.................	10.2	11.5	11.1	13.7	20.7	.9	....	....
Alcoholic beverages........	2.0	2.3	2.6	3.7	....	....	.5	....
Tobacco products..........	2.8	2.2	2.7	1.9	.8	....	....	....
Public utilities.............	1.1	....	....	....	....	....	....	....
Other sales and gross-receipts taxes...................	2.8	4.5	4.4	3.8	6.8	8.9	14.1	14.6
Property....................	1.8	1.9	2.2	3.8	12.9	25.6	37.2	42.7
Motor vehicle and operators' licenses....................	4.8	5.6	5.5	6.3	13.2	11.2	1.3	....
Other taxes.................	6.0	6.9	6.4	6.9	13.7	15.6	26.9	24.0
Charges and miscellaneous general revenue........................	7.9	7.8	6.5	5.4	10.4	13.3	15.7	13.0
Liquor stores revenue...............	3.4	4.3	5.5	5.4	....	....	....	1.0
Insurance trust revenue.............	13.2	13.0	14.6	19.9	4.6	7.8	....	....

Source: See Table 3.

ated by other units of government than cities and are affected by general revenue patterns.

The survey of local revenues since 1902 (Table 6) brings out five facts:

First, since 1902 there has been a tremendous increase in the amount of revenue required by local governments. In 1902, local revenues were only $914,-000,000; in 1960 the sum was $37,527,-000,000—over forty times as much. This growth is characteristic of all types of government, as has been mentioned.

the federal government, which are also indicated in Table 6.

Third, although there has been a large increase in the amount of sales and gross-receipts taxes, the relative importance of these levies to local governments is still small. In comparison with some other taxes these are comparatively easy to administer. It should be added, too, that some local levies are in the nature of surcharges to be collected and remitted by the states, as is true, for example, in Illinois.

TABLE 5

COMPARISON OF NUMBER OF LOCAL UNITS, THEIR REVENUES, AND EXPENDITURES, 1957

Units	No. of Districts	Per Cent	Total Revenue (Millions)	Per Cent	Total Expenditures (Millions)	Per Cent
Counties..........	3,047	3.0	$ 5,743	19.5	$ 5,860	18.7
Cities.............	17,183	16.8	12,047	41.0	12,839	40.9
Townships.........	17,198	16.8	1,228	4.2	1,251	4.0
School districts.....	50,446	49.3	8,914	30.3	9,644	30.7
Special districts.....	14,405	14.1	1,475	5.0	1,795	5.7
Total..........	102,279	100.0	$29,407	100.0	$31,389	100.0

Source: *1957 Census of Governments*, Vol. III, *Governmental Finances*, No. 5; and *Compendium of Government Finances* (Department of Commerce, Bureau of the Census [July 1959]), pp. 1, 17, 19.

Second, the growth in intergovernmental revenues, or transfers, has been tremendous. The amount, including payments by both the federal and state governments, has risen from $56,000,-000 in 1902 to $9,951,000,000 in 1960. The percentage of these revenues has changed from a mere 6 per cent of total revenues to over 26.5 per cent. When over a fourth of local revenues represent payments for local functions from funds provided by other levels of government, a drastic change in the pattern of financing public services has taken place! This is the most important change that has taken place in local public finance. Similarly, attention is called to the growth in payments from

Fourth, in spite of the fact that the amounts collected from the property tax continue to rise, and that it is still the largest single source of local revenue, the relative importance of the property tax has declined. In 1960, local property taxes aggregated over $16,-094,000,000 and provided 42.9 per cent of total revenues. In 1902, the localities depended upon this tax for 68.2 per cent of their revenues. In earlier years the reliance on this tax was even greater though the actual statistics were never gathered. The decline in the relative importance in this tax is the direct consequence of the growth of other forms of revenue and of other taxes. It is believed that property tax levies are the

TABLE 6

TABLE 6
LOCAL REVENUES, 1902–60

Sources of Revenue	1960	1957	1952	1942	1932	1922	1913	1902
	Amount (Millions)							
Total..........................	$37,527	$28,896	$19,398	$8,114	$6,192	$4,148	$1,755	$914
Total general revenue (direct and intergovernmental)...............	33,274	25,406	16,952	7,122	5,690	3,866	1,637	854
Intergovernmental revenue:								
From federal government.........	590	343	237	56	10	9	6	4
From state governments..........	9,361	7,196	5,044	1,780	801	312	91	52
Revenue from local sources........	27,576	21,357	14,117	6,278	5,381	3,827	1,658	858
General revenue from local sources.	23,323	17,866	11,671	5,286	4,879	3,545	1,540	798
Taxes.......................	18,386	14,286	9,466	4,625	4,274	3,069	1,308	704
Individual income............	254	191	85	27	......	......	......	......
Corporation income..........	......	......	8	3	......	......	......	......
Sales and gross receipts.......	1,339	1,031	627	133	26	20	3	......
Property....................	16,094	12,385	8,282	4,273	4,159	2,973	1,192	624
Other taxes, including licenses.	698	679	465	189	89	76	113	80
Charges and miscellaneous general revenue..................	4,938	3,580	2,205	661	605	476	232	94
Utility revenue..................	3,570	2,944	2,071	887	463	266	116	60
Water supply systems...........	......	1,235	839	439	317	175	99	56
Electric power systems..........	......	1,011	683	251	111	72	16	3
Transit systems................	......	541	479	170	25	13	......	......
Gas supply systems.............	......	157	70	27	10	6	1	1
Liquor stores revenue.............	134	118	113	17	......	......	......	......
Insurance trust revenue...........	549	429	262	88	39	16	2	......
Employee retirement.............	......	423	256	80	39	16	2	......
Unemployment compensation...	......	6	5	8	......	......	......	......
	Per Cent of Total							
Total..........................	100.0	100.0	100.0	100.0	100.0	100.0	100.0	100.0
Total general revenue (direct and intergovernmental)...............	88.7	87.9	87.4	87.8	91.9	93.2	93.3	93.4
Intergovernmental revenue:								
From federal government.........	1.6	1.2	1.2	.7	.2	.2	.3	.4
From state governments..........	24.9	24.9	26.0	21.9	12.9	7.5	5.2	5.7
Revenue from local sources.........	73.5	73.9	72.8	77.4	86.9	92.3	94.5	93.9
General revenue from local sources.	62.1	61.9	60.2	65.1	78.8	85.5	87.7	87.3
Taxes.......................	49.0	49.4	48.8	57.0	69.0	74.0	74.5	77.0
Individual income............	.7	.7	.4	.3	......	......	......	......
Corporation income..........	......	......	.1	.0	......	......	......	......
Sales and gross receipts.......	3.6	3.6	3.2	1.6	.4	.5	.2	......
Property....................	42.9	42.8	42.7	52.7	67.2	71.7	67.9	68.3
Other taxes, including licenses.	1.8	2.3	2.4	2.3	1.4	1.8	6.4	8.7
Charges and miscellaneous general revenue..................	13.1	12.4	11.4	8.1	9.8	11.5	13.2	10.3
Utility revenue..................	9.5	10.2	10.7	10.9	7.5	6.4	6.6	6.6
Water supply systems...........	......	4.3	4.3	5.4	5.1	4.2	5.6	6.1
Electric power systems..........	......	3.5	3.5	3.1	1.8	1.7	.9	.3
Transit systems................	......	1.9	2.5	2.1	.4	.3	......	......
Gas supply systems.............	......	.5	.4	.3	.2	.1	.1	.1
Liquor stores revenue.............	.4	.4	.6	.2	......	......	......	......
Insurance trust revenue...........	1.5	1.4	1.3	1.1	.6	.4	.1	......
Employee retirement.............	......	1.4	1.3	1.0	.6	.4	.1	......
Unemployment compensation...	......	.0	.0	.1	......	......	......	......

Source: See Table 3.

primary support of libraries and special library districts, but corroborating facts on library income are lacking to support this impression.

If the revenues of cities are tabulated, using Census size classes for the three groups of cities having populations of less than 100,000, the importance of the property tax in the reve-

of their revenues from the property tax. Utility revenues had almost twice the relative importance to cities with less than 25,000 as compared with cities having 50,000–100,000 inhabitants. The ease of collecting these charges may have something to do with this situation.

Fifth, utility revenues also loom

TABLE 7

REVENUES OF CITIES, BY POPULATION SIZE CLASSES, 1960

SOURCES OF REVENUE	AMOUNTS (IN MILLIONS)				PER CENT OF TOTAL			TOTAL
	Cities 50,000–99,999	Cities 25,000–49,999	Cities Less than 25,000	Total	Cities 50,000–99,999	Cities 25,000–49,999	Cities Less than 25,000	
Total..........................	$1,406	$1,284	$2,973	$2,690	100.0	100.0	99.9	9.9
General revenue.................	1,154	1,001	2,014	2,155	82.1	77.9	67.7	80.1
Taxes......................	729	600	1,083	1,329	51.8	46.8	36.4	49.4
Property...................	600	487	844	1,087	42.7	37.9	28.4	40.4
General sales and gross receipts	36	34	60	70	2.6	2.6	2.0	2.6
Selective sales and gross receipts	32	32	51	64	2.3	2.5	1.7	2.4
Other taxes, including licenses.	60	48	128	108	4.3	3.7	4.3	4.0
Intergovernmental revenue......	206	172	411	378	14.7	13.4	13.8	14.1
From State government only..	174	143	344	317	12.4	11.1	11.6	11.8
Charges and miscellaneous general revenue.................	219	228	520	447	15.6	17.7	17.5	16.6
Current charges.............	147	151	281	298	10.5	11.8	9.4	11.1
Special assessments.........	28	36	112	64	2.0	2.8	3.8	2.4
Other and unallocable........	44	41	127	85	3.1	3.2	4.3	3.1
Utility revenue..................	234	273	902	507	16.6	21.3	30.3	18.8
Water supply systems..........	133	136	400	269	9.4	10.6	13.4	10.0
Other utilities.................	101	137	502	238	7.2	10.7	16.9	8.8
Employee retirement revenue......	13	7	6	9	0.4	0.3	1.7	0.7
All other.......................	5	4	51	9	0.4	0.3	1.7	0.3

Source: *Compendium of City Government Finances in 1960* (Department of Commerce, Bureau of the Census, G-CF60, No. 2), p. 8.

nues of these cities decreases as population diminishes. I think that this is contrary to prevailing opinions. As shown in Table 7, the property tax in 1960 accounted for 42.7 per cent of total revenues in cities from 50,000 to 99,999 inhabitants, 38 per cent in cities of 25,000 to 49,999 inhabitants, and 28 per cent in cities with less than 25,000 inhabitants. The cities from 25,000 to 100,000 received 40 per cent

larger as a source of local revenue in the last ten years than in the years following 1902 (Table 6). In fact, the percentage contribution of utility revenues tended to decline from 1902 to 1942. Since that date they have tended to increase.

The same general trends in revenues are present if, instead of taking all local governments, cities alone are considered. Comparisons of city revenues for

1930, 1950, and 1960 are shown in
Table 8.[11] The decline of the property
tax, the rise in sales taxes, the growth
in intergovernmental revenues and in
utility charges all plainly appear. Liquor
store revenues show as a new class of
income for 1960.

REVENUES OF SELECTED CITIES

There is also a wide variation among
the revenue sources for individual

Table 9. The revenue patterns of the
states that contain these cities show
little uniformity. Some rely heavily on
property taxes, others on sales taxes,
some on personal and corporate income
taxes. These variations show up for the
cities. Stamford, Connecticut, depended
on property taxes for over 80 per cent
of its revenues in 1960. Huntsville, Alabama, received only 6.5 per cent of its
revenue from this source. San Bernar-

TABLE 8

GENERAL REVENUES OF CITIES, 1930–60

TYPES OF REVENUE	1960		1950		1930	
	Revenue (Millions)	Per Cent	Revenue (Millions)	Per Cent	Revenue (Millions)	Per Cent
Property taxes	$ 5,197	34.8	$2,324	40.2	$2,196*	64.2
Sales and gross-receipts taxes	1,217	8.2	415	7.2		
Licenses and other taxes	695	4.7	289	5.0	177†	5.2
Intergovernmental revenues	2,321	15.5	908	15.7	164	4.8
Charges and miscellaneous‡	2,217	14.9	481	8.3	510§	14.9
Utility revenues‖	2,790	18.7	1,039	18.0	339	9.9
Liquor stores revenue	71	0.5				
Insurance trust revenue	407	2.7	327#	5.6	33	1.0
Total	$14,915	100.0	$5,783	100.0	$3,419	100.0

* Receipts from general property and special property taxes.
† Includes business license taxes, non-business license taxes (dogs, general licenses and permits), and special taxes.
‡ Includes current charges, interest earnings, special assessments, sale of property, and other charges.
§ Includes poll taxes; receipts from special assessments; fines, forfeits, and escheats; revenue from highway privileges; rent of investment properties; interest; earnings of general departments; and donations by private persons and corporations.
‖ Includes water supply, electric power, transit, and gas supply systems.
Contributions to trust funds and enterprises.
Source: *Financial Statistics of Cities 1930* (Department of Commerce, Bureau of the Census); *Compendium of City Government Revenues in 1950;* and *Compendium of City Government Revenues in 1960.*

cities. Fifteen cities having populations
of 50,000 to 100,000 were selected at
random from fifteen states. The sources
of revenue for these cities are shown in

[11] Unfortunately changes in Census classifications
and their treatment of data make comparison somewhat difficult, but an effort has been made to put
the data for 1930 in a form that permits comparison with 1960. The 1930 *Financial Statistics
of Cities* covers cities having a population of 30,000
and over. The *Compendium of City Government
Finances in 1950* deals with cities of over 25,000
inhabitants, while the *Compendium* for 1960 includes cities with less than 25,000 inhabitants.

dino, California, depended on general
sales and gross-receipts taxes for over
22 per cent of its revenue. Twelve
of the cities in Table 9 received nothing
at all from general sales taxes—or too
little to be recorded. Selective sales
taxes were productive of revenues in
seven cities; eight places did not use
them. Other taxes, mainly licenses, provided 35.6 per cent of the revenues
for Lexington, Kentucky, 27 per cent
for Springfield, Ohio, 13 per cent for

TABLE 9

SOURCES OF REVENUE OF FIFTEEN SELECTED CITIES, 1960

Revenue (Thousands)

Population and Revenues	Huntsville, Ala.	San Bernardino, Calif.	Pueblo, Colo.	Stamford, Conn.	Wilmington, Del.	Muncie, Ind.	Cedar Rapids, Iowa	Lexington, Ky.	Brockton, Mass.	Pontiac, Mich.	Bloomington, Minn.	Troy, N.Y.	Springfield, Ohio	Reading, Pa.	Racine, Wis.
Population	72,365	91,222	91,181	92,712	95,827	68,603	92,035	62,810	72,813	82,233	50,498	67,492	82,723	98,177	89,144
Total	$11,807	$8,063	$6,227	$15,362	$19,645	$3,142	$7,588	$6,323	$14,710	$13,053	$3,576	$5,928	$8,313	$5,929	$15,832
General revenue	4,248	6,667	4,681	15,221	17,824	3,113	6,334	6,185	13,975	12,139	3,540	5,382	7,370	4,414	14,671
Taxes	2,927	4,102	3,116	12,528	8,259	1,806	4,774	4,348	8,543	3,818	1,162	3,975	3,167	3,409	8,948
Property	767	1,631	1,892	12,414	7,072	1,769	4,624	1,972	8,420	3,731	1,055	3,645	922	2,518	8,793
General sales and gross receipts	985	1,824	757												
Selective sales and gross receipts	554	92	288		96			125				281		112	
Other taxes, including licenses	621	555	179	114	1,091	37	150	2,251	123	87	107	49	2,245	779	155
Intergovernmental revenue	272	888	446	1,748	6,129	643	496	719	4,508	1,701	346	527	778	373	4,456
From state government only	86	884	440	1,599	6,106	593	496	32	4,396	1,512	346	517	778	360	4,105
Charges and miscellaneous general revenue	1,049	1,677	1,119	945	3,436	664	1,064	1,118	924	6,620	2,032	880	3,425	632	1,267
Current charges	431	1,382	464	684	2,870	616	922	966	725	5,893	350	780	2,980	331	671
Special assessments	141	51	246	80	13		142	15	66	413	1,472	9	66	3	282
Other and unallocable	477	244	409	181	553	48		137	133	314	210	91	379	298	314
Utility revenue	7,559	1,396	1,477		1,642		1,147		517	520	36	543	892	1,390	1,136
Water supply systems	1,028	1,396	1,477		1,642		1,147		517	520	36	543	892	1,390	1,136
Other utilities	6,531														
Employee retirement revenue			69	141	179	29	107	138	218	394		3	51	125	25

Source: *City Government Finances in 1960* (Department of Commerce, Bureau of the Census), pp. 10–41.

26

TABLE 9—Continued

Population and Revenues	Hunts-ville, Ala.	San Bernar-dino, Calif.	Pueblo, Colo.	Stam-ford, Conn.	Wilming-ton, Del.	Muncie, Ind.	Cedar Rapids, Iowa	Lexing-ton, Ky.	Brock-ton, Mass.	Pontiac, Mich.	Bloom-ington, Minn.	Troy, N.Y.	Spring-field, Ohio	Read-ing, Pa.	Racine, Wis.
Population	72,365	91,222	91,181	92,712	95,827	68,603	92,035	62,810	72,813	82,233	50,498	67,492	82,723	98,177	89,144
Per Cent of Total															
Total	100.0	100.0	100.0	100.0	100.0	100.0	100.0	100.0	100.0	100.0	100.0	100.0	100.0	99.9	100.0
General revenue	36.0	82.7	75.2	99.1	90.7	99.1	83.5	97.8	95.0	93.0	99.0	90.8	88.7	74.4	92.7
Taxes	24.8	50.9	50.0	81.5	42.0	57.5	62.9	68.7	58.1	29.2	32.5	67.1	38.1	57.5	56.5
Property	6.5	20.2	30.4	80.8	36.0	56.3	60.9	31.2	57.2	28.6	29.5	61.5	11.1	42.5	55.5
General sales and gross receipts	8.3	22.6	12.1	.....	.....	.....	.....	.....	.....	.....	.....	.....	.....	.....	.....
Selective sales and gross receipts	4.7	1.1	4.6	.....	0.5	.....	2.0	1.9	.....	.....	.....	4.7	.....	1.9	.....
Other taxes, including licenses	5.3	6.9	2.9	0.7	5.5	1.2	.....	35.6	0.8	0.6	3.0	0.8	27.0	13.1	1.0
Intergovernmental revenue	2.3	11.0	7.2	11.4	31.2	20.5	6.5	11.4	30.6	13.0	9.7	8.9	9.4	6.3	28.1
From state government only	0.7	11.0	7.1	10.4	31.1	18.9	6.5	0.5	29.8	11.6	9.7	8.7	9.4	6.3	28.1
Charges and miscellaneous general revenue	8.9	20.8	18.0	6.1	17.5	21.1	14.0	17.7	6.3	50.8	56.8	14.8	41.2	6.1	25.9
Current charges	3.7	17.1	7.4	4.4	14.6	19.6	12.1	15.3	4.9	45.1	9.8	13.2	35.8	10.6	8.0
Special assessments	1.2	0.6	3.9	0.5	0.1	.....	.....	0.2	0.4	3.2	41.1	0.1	0.8	5.6	4.2
Other and unallocable	4.3	3.0	6.6	1.2	2.8	1.5	1.9	2.2	0.9	2.4	5.9	1.5	4.6	0.0	1.8
Utility revenue	64.0	17.3	23.7	.....	8.4	.....	15.1	.....	3.5	4.0	1.0	9.1	10.7	5.0	2.0
Water supply systems	8.7	17.3	23.7	.....	8.4	.....	15.1	.....	3.5	4.0	1.0	9.1	10.7	23.4	7.2
Other utilities	55.3	.....	.....	.....	.....	.....	.....	.....	.....	.....	.....	.....	.....	23.4	7.2
Employee retirement revenue	.....	1.1	1.1	0.9	0.9	0.9	1.4	2.2	1.5	3.0	.....	0.1	0.6	2.1	0.1

Reading, Pennsylvania, and relatively little in the other places. Intergovernmental transfers provided over 31 per cent of the receipts of Wilmington, Delaware, 30.6 per cent for Brockton, Massachusetts, and 28.1 per cent for Racine, Wisconsin. The lowest amount of transfers was in Huntsville, Alabama, with 2.3 per cent from this source, but if the state's own payments alone were counted it would have amounted to only 0.7 per cent. Only the Commonwealth of Kentucky contributed less—0.5 per cent to Lexington. Yet, thanks to the federal government, that city received 11.4 per cent of its revenues by way of intergovernmental transfers. Neither Iowa nor Pennsylvania did much for Cedar Rapids (6.5 per cent) or Reading (6.1 per cent). Miscellaneous charges, which include such items as parking meter nickels and pennies, special assessments, interest earnings, sale of properties and other minor sources, provided Bloomington, Minnesota, with almost 57 per cent of its revenue—not a very sturdy base for a growing suburb. Special assessments alone—levied most probably for street or sewer construction—provided 41.1 per cent of Bloomington's revenue. This reflects boomtown activities, especially housing of some type.[12] Utility revenues provided Huntsville, Alabama, with 64 per cent of its funds and Pueblo, Colorado, with 24 per cent. Thus in the fifteen cities shown in Table 9 property taxes and intergovernmental transfers constituted the generally most important sources of local revenue.

If a similar group of cities is selected

from a single state for the analysis of revenue sources a similar diversity is evidenced. Such a sample is provided by the fifteen cities in Illinois having over 50,000 inhabitants. Illinois, too, is not one of the "enlightened" states with a model modern or even tolerably equitable tax system.[13] Illinois belongs to the group of states that conform to Adam Smith's admonition: "when the wisest government has exhausted all the proper subjects of taxation it must, in cases of urgent necessity, have recourse to improper ones."[14] Of course, Smith would not have characterized Illinois as being one of the wisest of governments nor as having been reduced to the extremity of using poor taxes. Illinois has used them traditionally and for normal purposes. Their present adequacy is now being tested by the needs of the state for current funds. These remarks apply also to many other states.

Property taxes were the major source of revenue for the fifteen Illinois cities in Table 10, but the relative importance of this tax was not as high as might be imagined. Peoria depended more on the property tax than other Illinois cities but received only 55 per cent of its revenue from this source. Springfield put least dependence upon the property tax of the large Illinois cities—18.7

---

[12] Bloomington does not operate its own public library but is served by a branch of the Hennepin County (Minneapolis) Library (7,500 volumes in 1960).

[13] In 1960 the state of Illinois received total tax revenues of $836,372,000, of which 82.5 per cent came from sales taxes. The general sales tax produced 44.8 per cent of the total, the motor fuel tax 16.9 per cent, tobacco products 5.9 per cent, public utilities 5.8 per cent, alcoholic beverages 3.8 per cent. Motor vehicle licenses produced 12 per cent; death and gift taxes 2.6 per cent, and the property tax which the state has abandoned to the local governments, 0.1 per cent. Minor sources account for the remainder (*Compendium of State Government Finances in 1960* [Department of Commerce, Bureau of the Census], pp. 13–15).

[14] *Wealth of Nations* (1776), Bk. V, chap. iii.

TABLE 10

SOURCES OF REVENUE OF FIFTEEN ILLINOIS CITIES, 1960

Population and Revenues	Aurora	Berwyn	Chicago	Cicero	Decatur	East St. Louis	Evanston	Joliet	Oak Park	Peoria	Rockford	Rock Island	Skokie	Springfield	Waukegan
Population	63,715	54,224	3,550,404	69,130	78,004	81,712	79,283	66,780	61,093	103,162	126,706	51,863	59,364	83,271	55,719
					Revenue (Millions)										
Total	$3,540	$2,724	$408,864	$5,528	$4,028	$5,027	$6,717	$3,682	$4,193	$7,146	$8,417	$4,023	$3,868	$9,147	$3,539
General revenue	2,798	2,012	342,170	4,328	2,953	4,955	5,283	2,513	3,312	7,014	6,630	3,407	2,823	4,376	2,781
Taxes	2,100	1,549	246,770	3,203	1,963	2,888	3,949	1,833	2,325	5,333	4,465	1,820	2,095	2,662	1,961
Property	1,361	721	148,153	2,353	1,144	1,957	2,771	961	1,452	3,908	2,666	1,249	1,105	1,709	1,196
General sales and gross receipts	524	517	22,627	440	……	496	567	597	554	990	1,005	315	545	697	488
Selective sales and gross receipts	20	8	33,941	17	626	49	19	20	14	217	197	9	14	26	……
Other taxes, including licenses	195	303	42,049	393	193	386	592	255	305	218	597	247	431	230	277
Intergovernmental revenue. From state government only	326	213	56,160	589	504	211	472	427	427	787	670	91	123	552	262
Charges and miscellaneous general revenue	310	213	43,609	589	502	211	472	423	425	712	628	71	123	424	262
Current charges	372	250	39,240	536	486	1,856	862	253	560	894	1,495	1,496	605	1,162	558
Special assessments	223	87	21,921	293	210	1,620	430	128	423	367	693	1,067	61	818	129
Other and unallocable	56	104	5,742	4	222	……	125	42	13	219	447	131	459	87	204
	93	59	11,577	239	54	236	307	83	124	308	355	298	85	257	225
Utility revenue	693	680	40,128	1,139	1,023	……	1,339	1,124	806	……	1,675	577	1,045	4,719	715
Water supply systems	693	680	40,128	1,139	1,023	……	1,339	1,124	806	……	1,675	577	1,045	1,263	715
Other utilities	……	……	……	……	……	……	……	……	……	……	……	……	……	3,456	……
Employee retirement revenue	49	32	26,566	61	52	72	95	45	75	132	112	39	52	52	43

Source: *City Government Finances in 1960* (Department of Commerce, Bureau of the Census), pp. 18–19.

TABLE 10—Continued

Population and Revenues	Aurora	Berwyn	Chicago	Cicero	Decatur	East St. Louis	Evanston	Joliet	Oak Park	Peoria	Rockford	Rock Island	Skokie	Springfield	Waukegan
Population	63,715	54,224	3,550,404	69,130	78,004	81,712	79,283	66,780	61,093	103,162	126,706	51,863	59,364	83,271	55,719
Per Cent of Total															
Total	100.0	100.0	100.0	100.0	100.0	100.0	100.0	100.0	100.0	100.0	100.0	100.0	100.0	100.0	100.0
General revenue	79.0	73.9	83.7	78.3	73.3	98.6	78.7	68.3	80.0	98.2	78.8	84.7	73.0	47.8	78.5
Taxes	59.3	56.9	60.4	57.9	48.7	57.5	58.8	49.8	55.4	74.6	53.0	45.2	54.2	29.1	55.4
Property	38.4	26.5	36.2	42.6	28.4	38.9	41.3	26.1	34.6	54.7	31.7	31.1	28.6	18.7	33.8
General sales and gross receipts	14.8	19.0	5.5	7.9		9.9	8.4	16.2	13.2	13.9	11.9	7.8	14.1	7.6	13.8
Selective sales and gross receipts	.6	.3	8.3	.3	15.5	1.0	.3	.6	.3	3.0	2.3	.2	.4	.3	
Other taxes, including licenses	5.5	11.1	10.3	7.1	4.8	7.7	8.8	6.9	7.3	3.0	7.1	6.1	11.1	2.5	7.8
Intergovernmental revenue	9.2	7.8	13.7	10.7	12.5	4.2	7.0	11.6	10.2	11.0	8.0	2.3	3.2	6.0	7.4
From state government only	8.6	7.8	10.6	10.7	12.5	4.2	7.0	11.5	10.2	1.0	7.5	1.8	3.2	4.6	7.4
Charges and miscellaneous general revenue	10.5	9.2	9.6	9.7	12.1	36.9	12.8	6.9	13.4	12.5	17.8	37.2	15.6	12.7	15.8
Current charges	6.3	3.2	5.4	5.3	5.2	32.2	6.4	3.5	10.1	5.1	8.2	26.5	1.6	8.9	3.6
Special assessments	1.6	3.8	1.4	.1	5.5		1.8	1.1	.3	3.1	5.3	7.4	11.8	1.0	5.8
Other and unallocable	2.6	2.2	2.8	4.3	1.3	4.7	4.6	2.3	3.0	4.3	4.2		2.2	2.8	6.4
Utility revenue	19.6	24.9	9.8	20.6	25.4		19.9	30.5	19.2		19.9	14.3	27.0	51.6	20.2
Water supply systems	19.6	24.9	9.8	20.6	25.4		19.9	30.5	19.2		19.9	14.3	27.0	13.8	20.2
Other utilities														37.8	
Employee retirement revenue	1.4	1.2	6.5	1.0	1.3	1.4	1.4	1.2	1.8	1.9	1.3	1.0		.6	1.2

per cent—but received over 51 per cent of its revenue from its municipally owned utilities. Sales taxes provided Berwyn with 19 per cent of its revenues. Aurora, Joliet, Oak Park, Peoria, Skokie, and Waukegan all received from 13 to 16 per cent of their revenues from sales taxes. Intergovernmental revenues were of less importance to practically all cities in Illinois than property and sales taxes—and of far less importance than the average in the cities of the nation.[15] Chicago and Cicero, however, received more from intergovernmental transfers than from sales taxes. Excluding Chicago, the largest relative amount of transfers was in Decatur where intergovernmental payments amounted to 12.5 per cent of total revenues. They were smallest in Rock Island (2.3 per cent) and Skokie (3.2 per cent). Six cities (Berwyn, Cicero, East St. Louis, Evanston, Skokie, and Waukegan) received transfers only from the state government. Only nominal additions were received by Decatur, Joliet, and Oak Park. Substantial revenues from utility charges were received by Springfield, Aurora, Berwyn, Cicero, Decatur, Evanston, Joliet, Oak Park, Rockford, Skokie, and Waukegan—ranging from 19.2 to 30.5 per cent, with over 51 per cent for Springfield—from utility charges. East St. Louis and Peoria reported no revenues from this source—doubtless due to the dominance of privately owned utilities.

RELATION BETWEEN CITY REVENUES
AND PUBLIC LIBRARY EXPENDITURES

It is interesting to compare the revenues of the thirty cities in Tables 9 and 10 with the expenditures of the public libraries in these same places (Table 11).[16] The twenty-one cities for which data on library expenditures are available spend on the average 2.7 per cent of city revenues on such expenditures. What the proper relationship should be, or what is a reasonably acceptable ratio, the author does not know. In the nine cities in that number of states (Table 9) public libraries received 2.2 per cent of city revenues; twelve of the large public libraries in Illinois received 3.3 per cent of city revenues. In Decatur, Illinois, library expenditures amounted to 7.2 per cent of the revenues of the city government. In Muncie, Indiana, the public library expenditures were 6.2 per cent of city revenues. Six city libraries spent less than 2 per cent of the revenues of the cities in which they were located (Table 11). The libraries in Evanston and Oak Park, Illinois, spent a little more than 4 per cent. It was shown in Table 2 that in 1960 libraries accounted for only 1.2 per cent of the expenditures of city governments in the United States.

The relatively slight impact of public library expenditures on city revenues may have caused those interested in libraries to feel that public library services would be better supported if library boards (or their governing bodies) were completely independent of other local governments. Such a divorcement has been urged in many quarters, but the author knows of no evidence to prove the advantage one way or the other. Whatever the administrative machinery—be it a sepa-

[15] Cf. Tables 6, 7, and 10.

[16] Information is not available to compare city revenues and public library revenues, but it is believed that there is little difference between revenues and operating expenses in most places. Capital outlays have been excluded since many buildings are constructed with the proceeds of bond issues.

rate board or an agency of the government itself—the funds for library support must either come from property tax levies specifically authorized for the purpose and subject to tax-limit laws, or from general local revenue sources, whatever they are, with library (department) earnings, income from endowments, gifts, and intergovernmental revenues added. Nothing can be said on principle for library support by special-purpose taxes unrelated to other local needs, or for exempting any type of local public service from the budgetary appraisal of its worth. Even where authority exists for library boards to fix their own property tax levies for support, the tax limits imposed by gen-

TABLE 11

OPERATING EXPENDITURES OF PUBLIC LIBRARIES COMPARED WITH
CITY REVENUES, SELECTED CITIES, 1960

CITIES	TOTAL CITY REVENUES (IN MILLIONS)*	PUBLIC LIBRARY OPERATING EXPENSES	
		Amount†	Per Cent of City Revenues
Huntsville, Alabama............	$11,807	....	....
San Bernardino, California......	8,063	$181,447	2.3
Pueblo, Colorado..............	6,227	N.a.	....
Stamford, Connecticut.........	15,362	322,841	2.1
Wilmington, Delaware.........	19,645	256,511	1.3
Muncie, Indiana..............	3,142	194,616	6.2
Cedar Rapids, Iowa...........	7,588	244,775	3.2
Lexington, Kentucky..........	6,323	N.a.	....
Brockton, Massachusetts.......	14,710	151,746	1.0
Pontiac, Michigan.............	13,053	142,285	1.1
Bloomington, Minnesota.......	3,576	N.a.	....
Troy, New York..............	5,928	72,030	1.2
Springfield, Ohio.............	8,313	N.a.	....
Reading, Pennsylvania.........	5,929	165,909	2.8
Racine, Wisconsin............	15,832	N.a.	....
Average.................	....	....	2.2
Illinois cities:			
Aurora....................	$ 3,540	$135,050	3.8
Berwyn...................	2,724	64,789	2.4
Chicago..................	408,864	N.a.	....
Cicero...................	5,528	80,780	1.5
Decatur..................	4,028	288,879	7.2
East St. Louis.............	5,027	65,242	1.3
Evanston.................	6,717	277,422	4.1
Joliet....................	3,682	119,978	3.3
Oak Park.................	4,193	170,895	4.1
Peoria...................	7,146	N.a.	....
Rockford.................	8,417	N.a.	....
Rock Island..............	4,023	93,029	2.3
Skokie...................	3,868	128,104	3.3
Springfield...............	9,147	278,992	3.1
Waukegan................	3,539	128,198	3.6
Average.................	....	....	3.3

* *Compendium of City Government Finances in 1960* (Department of Commerce, Bureau of the Census), Table 5, pp. 10 ff.

† *Library Statistics* (Department of Health, Education, and Welfare, OE-15034 [March, 1962]), pp. 6–15. (No statistics in this publication for Chicago, Peoria, and Rockford.)

eral laws represent a rough appraisal of the worth of these services compared with others for which complementary levies are likewise permitted. In one case local officials and budget officers set the value of the services; in the other it is done by a legislative assembly by general statutes. In both cases the public's estimate of the need and worth of public libraries will over the years determine the amounts made available for this service. These estimates vary over time and from place to place. Some communities want more and better library services if they can get them or pay for them; others may not. Local officials are assumed to be more responsive to these demands than state legislators or congressmen.

The position of the library as an educational institution raises the question as to whether or not public libraries should be integrated with the educational system. This does not mean that they should be run by school boards but rather that library boards might be set up with general responsibility to school authorities and with school revenues, such as were appropriated, flowing into library budgets. These administrative arrangements are anathema to some library authorities and probably to some school officials as well, but the fountain of educational funds has run freely and in substantial volume. Nor can it be denied that much might be gained in terms of improved physical facilities if library and school systems planned their needs together and worked more closely in providing educational services than they do now. Perhaps greater support for libraries could be realized more quickly this way—or with less difficulty —remembering that the supporters of education are numerous and that their pressures for appropriations have been effective. The close connection between schools and libraries might make a profitable alliance for both. Their educational function provides a basis for union. Nevertheless the library—its friends, supporters, and officials—would have to prove its worth compared with other activities competing for a share of educational funds.

The integration of the public library as a part of the city government also has its champions. They believe that efficiency of administration is best achieved when all local activities are encompassed in a single local government. Claims for funds then are appraised by a single budget authority and share in the pool of revenues available for all. There is no doubt that funds will be better allocated according to need and to the demands of citizens by way of a unitary local government than if these decisions are scattered among a number of independent or semi-independent bodies with various and scattered means of support.

Whatever the administrative setup, not much support for any activity can be provided outside of the limits of the prevailing system of local revenues. Some *ad hoc* units are tied directly to designated taxes; some have been given only the right to spend their earnings; some are simply borrowing agencies. Such plans for financial support are often temporary, always precarious and ill suited to the continuing operation of normal public functions. They are not appropriate for public libraries or for any general departments of local government. Local support for these activities depends in the end upon the productivity of the prevailing revenue systems.

QUEST FOR MUNICIPAL REVENUES

The raising of revenues for local governments is no longer a simple matter. The sums required are large. The power of local units to impose taxes for their own support is complicated by constitutional jurisdictional problems woven into our political framework when the loose federation of states united to form our national government. The complexities of our economic system with its territorial specialization of industry and trade that respects neither state nor municipal boundary lines add other difficulties to the situation. Even the division of labor in connection with specialized tax administration places small political units, such as cities, at a further disadvantage. They find it increasingly difficult to employ competent tax collectors.

Under our constitutional system the states are sovereign. The most effective accompaniment of that sovereignty, moreover, is the power to tax. The states have unlimited taxing powers, save as they have imposed limitations upon themselves in their own state constitutions or have delegated their powers to other governments. The taxing powers of the federal government were delegated to it expressly, or by implication, by the states, and fortunate it was that the taxing powers so delegated were both broad in the legal sense and highly productive of revenues as well. Otherwise, our national government could not have withstood the strain of recurrent wars and national crises; nor could it have met the increasing financial demands for extensions of federal services and assistance.

Local governments, by contrast, have only those taxing powers given them by the states. The housekeeping services performed by these local governments were once the most important of all public services to citizens, excepting, perhaps, provision for national security. Yet, in many decades of our national life, these military endeavors did not loom large. So it was that local functions for many decades were favored over those of other governments and experienced no financial difficulties.

In defraying the cost of public services, local units not only suffer from a legal handicap but also from the natural difficulty of trying to tax persons, property, and business located in small but not self-contained geographical areas. Seldom have the boundary lines of local tax jurisdictions confined the taxable capacities located there. Trade and business have moved freely across jurisdictional lines. People, at the slightest provocation, have been able to move away. Mobile property, business, and factories have been located beyond city or other corporate limits. Evasion of many local taxes has been easy, and the local tax collector has been at a disadvantage compared with officials of the states and federal government, nor have they competed on even terms with the more skilful and better informed tax agents and attorneys of important taxpayers. In vain have many cities tried to reach the tax-paying ability of city wage-earners who live beyond their territorial boundaries.

Except in time of war there was seldom any strain on the American governmental finance system. For years the federal government relied too heavily on customs duties and internal revenues, while the state supported itself with surcharges (state levies) imposed upon local general property taxes. Gradually, the state and federal governments developed centrally administered taxes of their own, but the major source of local revenue has continued to be the general property tax. The continued pressure for increased public expenditures and the continued difficulties with administration, state as well as local, have made the property tax an inadequate prop for the support of local governments. Not only have futile attempts been made to bolster the property tax and minimize its inequalities, but rates have been increased, new taxes have been added, utility charges have been exploited, sewer rentals have been adopted, garbage collection fees have been imposed, parking meters have been installed, advertising space has been sold, and all manner of things have been done in an attempt to increase the productivity of local revenue measures. As the limits of "self-help" were reached, appeals were made to states for permission to impose local additions or local surcharges to state taxes. Increased state grants were sought as were increases in sharing the yields of state-administered taxes.

Over the years such revenues encompassed under the rubric "intergovernmental revenues" or "governmental transfers" have become important both to state and local units. These governments have often become dependent upon them—like alimony payments. However, practically all of these funds are available only for purposes selected by the grantors and are subject to conditions imposed by the grantors. Some grants require the matching of funds; others do not. Some are for purposes of primary interest to the governmental unit transferring the funds; others are of greater value to the receiver. Things of importance to units in one area may be marginal or of little moment to others, but since the transfers must be of uniform applicability their impact upon local finances varies from place to place. Few of the transfers are for unrestricted purposes or simply to meet general revenue requirements. Nevertheless, and in spite of the difficulties, the hope of providing adequate and reasonably good sources of municipal revenue lies in the development and extension of intergovernmental transfers. The governments with good and fiscally adequate revenue systems must utilize them for the benefit of subordinate units. After all it is not the units of government that are to be financed but services to citizens—whether this is done by one unit or another it is largely the same people who are supplied with public services. The citizens of the city are also the citizens of the state; the citizens of the states are likewise citizens of the nation. The balancing of payments among them, as well as the incidence of both benefits and taxes, is a complicated problem. But this should not prevent the proper extensions of intergovernmental transfers.

INTERGOVERNMENTAL REVENUES

The flow of funds from federal to local governments for 1960 is indicated in Table 12. In that year the federal government transferred $6,382,000,000 to the states; the local governments transferred $363,000,000 to the states. The states augmented federal contributions to transfer $9,361,000,000 to local governments; the federal government transferred directly to the localities $590,000,000.

FEDERAL GRANTS

Federal grants flow to the states through various departments and agencies that exercise supervision over their subsequent expenditure. Highways and public assistance are the two largest categories of federal aid and together accounted for over $4,757,000,000 of payments in fiscal 1961.[17] The total number of objects and purposes for which federal grants are made is a long one and includes payments to states for library services.

In 1956, Congress passed a law "to promote the further extension by the several states of public library services to rural areas without such services or with inadequate services."[18] An appro-

tion of the United States."[20] State allocations were to be spent under the supervision of the state library administration.[21] None of the money could be spent for buildings or the purchase of land.[22] The services provided also had to be free.[23]

Under this law federal grants for library services have been made since fiscal 1957, as shown in Table 13. Payments to the states in fiscal 1961 were over $7,400,000 and ranged from $341,396 for Pennsylvania to $11,079

TABLE 12

INTERGOVERNMENTAL REVENUES AND EXPENDITURES, 1960

SOURCE	AMOUNT (IN MILLIONS)		
	Federal	State	Local
Intergovernmental revenue............	....	$6,745	$9,951
From federal government...........	....	6,382	590
From states.................	....		9,361
From local governments...........	....	363	....
Intergovernmental expenditures....	$6,994	$9,283	$ 209
To states....................	6,352	....	209
To local governments...........	642	9,283	....

Source: *Summary of Governmental Finances in 1960* (Department of Commerce, Bureau of the Census, G-GF60, No. 1 [August 18, 1961]), pp. 14–15.

priation was authorized for fiscal 1957 "and for each of the four succeeding fiscal years the sum of $7,500,000" to be used in "making payments to the states" whose state plans for the extension of public library services to rural areas had the approval of the United States Commissioner of Education.[19] The allocation formula allotted $10,000 to the Virgin Islands and Guam, and $40,000 to each state plus "such part of the remainder as the rural population of state bears to the total rural popula-

for the Virgin Islands.[24] Between these limits every state, the District of Columbia excluded, received something. Perhaps the rural part of the District is cared for in the rural regions of surrounding Maryland, and Virginia. It is worth noting that some of the suburban developments in District-adjacent Maryland are still—for tax purposes— declared to be rural lands!

[20] *Ibid.*, Sec. 4 (*a*). Guam was added by later amendment, by Act of August 1, 1956 (cf. 20 U.S.C. 351).

[21] *Ibid.*, Sec. 5.

[22] *Ibid.*, Sec. 6.

[23] *Ibid.*, Sec. 5 (*a*) (5).

[24] *Annual Report of the Secretary of the Treasury, 1961*, pp. 675 ff.

[17] *Annual Report of the Secretary of the Treasury, 1961*, pp. 675 ff.

[18] Public Law 597, Act of July 31, 1956, 70 Stat. 293.

[19] *Ibid.*, Sec. 3.

Why federal aid for libraries should be limited—as the act now specifies—to rural extensions may well be queried. This may be only the beginning. Highway aid has grown from $78,000,000 in 1930 to $2,591,000,000 in 1961; public assistance from $329,000,000 in 1930 to $2,167,000,000 in 1961; payments to states for wildlife restoration have increased from $450,000 in 1940 to $15,-500,000 in 1961.[25] The trend, of course, is generally upward. Why urban taxpayers, who pay the bulk of federal taxes, should limit aid for library service to rural extension is hard to see. It may be part of the general plan for reducing urban standards of living while artificially raising incomes and standards of living for farmers, as is done under the various federal crop-control subsidies. Of course, urban taxpayers have the money and can reasonably be asked to improve rural library service, but why they have not, by the same federal aid, tried to improve the levels of library service in urban communities and especially in newly developed suburban communities is hard to imagine. As good a case can be made for this as for rural extension. Perhaps this is on the agenda for the future.

STATE PAYMENTS

The increase in state payments to local governments has been pointed out in previous paragraphs and tables. Attention has also been called to the fact that the state governments have transmitted to the localities far more than they have received from the federal government. In the years prior to 1960 they have passed along sometimes more than twice as much as they received, and in the early years when the totals were

small even more than that.[26] The largest state payments have always been for education, and only recently has public welfare exceeded highway payments. This historical evolution is shown in Table 14.

The intergovernmental payments made by the states include shared taxes (state-administered with division of yields), profits from state enterprises, such as liquor stores, grants-in-aid, direct appropriations for various reimbursements, and payments in lieu of taxes.[27] Like federal grants most of

TABLE 13

FEDERAL GRANTS FOR
LIBRARY SERVICES

Fiscal Year Ending June 30	Amount
1957	$ 1,440,000
1958	4,892,032
1959	5,362,445
1960	7,036,729
1961	7,414,221
Total	$26,145,427

Source: *Annual Reports of the Secretary of the Treasury on the State of the Finances* for the fiscal years shown.

the transfers are for specific purposes chosen by the state. They are made to the usual political units in the hierarchy, as shown in Table 15.

In terms of total intergovernmental payments school districts receive the largest amount; counties get more than cities; townships more than the special districts. Municipalities receive more than other units for general local government support, for public assistance other than the categorical programs, for non-highway transportation, and for miscellaneous purposes. Counties re-

[25] *Ibid.*

[26] See Tables 4 and 6. The supplementation of federal payments by states was clearly shown for 1960 in Table 13.

[27] For detailed statements for each state see *1957 Census of Governments, State Payments to Local Governments*, IV, No. 2, 11 ff.

ceive more than other units for the categorical public assistance programs, highways, health and hospitals, and natural resources. These divisions reflect allocations of government functions and administration among the cities and towns. Counties received over $1,500,000. Connecticut led the states in the amount of library aid with its expenditure of $24,597,000. New York was next with transfers of $2,231,000, of which $1,816,000 went to the New

TABLE 14

STATE INTERGOVERNMENTAL REVENUE AND EXPENDITURE,
BY FUNCTION, 1902–60

YEAR	INTER-GOVERN-MENTAL REVENUE	INTERGOVERNMENTAL EXPENDITURE					
		Total	Education	Highways	Public Welfare	Other Specified Purposes	Purposes Un-specified
		Amount (in Millions)					
1960	$6,745	$9,283	$5,300	$1,247	$1,483	$271	$982
1957	3,928	7,315	4,087	1,082	1,025	453	668
1952	2,485	5,044	2,523	728	976	268	549
1942	858	1,780	790	344	390	32	224
1932	267	801	398	229	28	6	140
1922	126	312	202	70	4	1	35
1913	16	91	82	4	....	....	5
1902	9	52	45	2	....	....	5
		Per Cent of Total					
1960		100	57.1	13.4	16.0	2.9	10.6
1957		100	55.9	14.8	14.0	6.2	9.1
1952		100	50.0	14.4	19.4	5.3	10.9
1942		100	44.4	19.3	21.9	1.8	12.6
1932		100	49.7	28.6	3.5	0.7	17.5
1922		100	64.8	22.4	1.3	0.3	11.2
1913		100	90.1	4.4	....	....	5.5
1902		100	86.5	3.9	....	....	9.6

Source: *Compendium of State Government Finances in 1960*, pp. 8, 10; *1957 Census o Governments*, IV, No. 3, 20–21.

units of government. Public libraries are probably affected by grants to all units except the special districts.

STATE PAYMENTS FOR LIBRARY AID

Among the local activities for which state payments are made are library services. In 1957, thirteen states made payments of $28,635,000 to local units for library assistance (Table 16). Of this amount over $26,000,000 went to York City Public Library. No other cities were assisted by New York State. In Maryland, library aid went to Baltimore as its only city, but Baltimore was given less than the small amount transferred to counties. Ohio extended its aid to cities and school districts but not to other units. The Census classified all of these aids as "educational." Why more states have not granted libraries assistance either di-

TABLE 15

STATE INTERGOVERNMENTAL EXPENDITURES, BY FUNCTION AND TYPE OF RECEIVING UNIT, 1957

State and Type of Receiving Government	Total	General Local Government Support	Specified Functions									
			Public Welfare				Education	Highways	Health and Hospitals	Non-Highway Transportation	Natural Resources	Miscellaneous and Combined
			Total	Public Assistance		Other						
				Categorical Programs	Other							
Amount (in Thousands)												
Total	$7,314,575	$667,774	$1,025,155	$831,944	$128,940	$64,271	$4,087,053	$1,082,574	$253,072	$8,823	$10,805	$179,319
Counties	2,019,676	194,542	707,545	616,524	56,607	34,414	227,430	693,451	148,583	1,073	8,427	38,625
Municipalities	1,480,071	361,855	293,973	195,062	69,113	29,798	320,584	296,378	93,865	5,876	625	106,915
Townships	270,388	77,546	23,637	20,358	3,220	59	62,456	92,598	8,756	100	......	5,295
School districts	3,520,068	31,131	......	......	......	......	3,476,583	......	......	......	......	12,354
Special districts	24,372	2,700	......	......	......	......	......	147	1,868	1,774	1,753	16,130
Per Cent of Total												
Total	99.9	100.0	100.0	99.9	100.0	99.9	100.0	99.9	100.0	100.0	100.0	100.0
Counties	27.6	29.1	69.0	74.1	43.9	53.5	5.6	64.0	58.7	12.2	77.8	21.5
Municipalities	20.2	54.2	28.7	23.4	53.6	46.3	7.8	27.4	37.1	66.6	5.8	59.6
Townships	3.7	11.6	2.3	2.4	2.5	0.1	1.5	8.5	3.5	1.1	......	3.0
School districts	48.1	4.7	......	......	......	......	85.1	......	......	......	......	6.9
Special districts	0.3	0.4	......	......	......	......	......	0.0	0.7	20.1	16.2	9.0

Source: 1957 Census of Governments, State Payments to Local Governments, IV, No. 2 (Department of Commerce, Bureau of the Census), 7.

TABLE 16

STATE PAYMENTS TO LOCAL GOVERNMENTS FOR LIBRARY AID, 1957

State	Distribution of Amounts Appropriated	Unit	Amount (in Thousands)
Arkansas	Population, at a specified rate per capita to counties maintaining library service.	Counties	$ 80
Connecticut	Specified rates per pupil in average daily attendance; applicable rate depending upon number of pupils.	Cities	8,720
		Towns	15,178
		School districts	699
Delaware	To school districts meeting minimum qualifications in a fixed ratio to revenue raised locally for library purposes but not to exceed stated maximum.	School districts	10
Maine	Fixed ratios to local expenditure, subject to a specified maximum amount per municipality.	Cities and towns	14
Maryland	At specified rate per capita of population.	City*	114
Michigan	(a) For establishment of new library up to specified maximum amount, (b) as reimbursement of salary of head librarian up to specified maximum amount, and (c) remainder on population basis among governments maintaining approved libraries and raising required local revenue.	Counties	155
		Cities	210
		Counties	55
		Townships	8
		School districts	55
Missouri	One-half in proportion to population and one-half on basis of equalization formula to supplement proceeds of specified local property tax levy in financing a specified per capita amount for library support.	Cities	101
New York	To counties (and New York City) with approved library systems (a) in fixed ratio to local expenditure for books, periodicals, and binding, limited to maximum amount per 1,000 population, (b) in fixed amount per county annually, and (c) in fixed amount per county at time library services are approved.	Counties	149
		City†	1,816
		Counties	415
North Carolina	Flat grants to qualified counties; remainder distributed to such counties in proportion to population.	Counties	390
Ohio	To supplement local revenue on basis of per capita revenue from local intangible property taxes.	Cities and school districts	160
Pennsylvania	Fixed ratio to local support for free county libraries.	Counties	169
Rhode Island	(a) To supplement salaries up to a specified maximum amount, and (b) for purchase of books, amount based on number of volumes held, but not to exceed a specified maximum amount per library.	Cities	20
Virginia	(a) For establishing a library, in proportion to population at specified rate per capita, subject to specified maximum per county, and (b) in fixed ratio to local expenditure in bringing services up to prescribed standards.	Cities	20
		Counties	97
Total amount			$28,635

* Baltimore only.   † New York City only.

Source: *1957 Census of Governments, State Payments to Local Governments*, IV, No. 2 (June, 1959), 11 ff.

rectly or as part of the educational system is not known. Perhaps the explanation is that library supporters and friends have not pressed their case for assistance. Or perhaps, it is because citizens do not think of the public library as an integral or essential part of the educational system of the state. Over the years the concept of the responsibility of the state for education has greatly enlarged. Surely the state can include in its educational standards minimum public library facilities available to everyone—not just to those in rural areas. If this is true, state payments for library aid should greatly increase in the years to come.

TRANSFER OF SERVICES

No analysis of local finances is complete without some consideration of the allocation of functions between various levels of government. This is not a revenue problem per se, but some revenue problems have been avoided by the transfer of specific functions between governments. Some states have taken over local functions in order to relieve local units of the burden of financing them. Likewise special or *ad hoc* units have been created to provide similar relief, as well as to avoid tax- or debt-limit laws. The effect of the assumption of local services by the state has been the same as if the state had transferred funds to local governments to defray these costs. North Carolina, for example, early took over highway construction and maintenance even later, of city streets on highway routes. Historically the development of state highways was undertaken not only "to go get the state [or the farmer] out of the mud" but to relieve local governments of impossibly large financial burdens. Public welfare payments by central govern-

ments and the state assumption of relief and public health functions have been of the same order. While the state will undoubtedly increase its assistance to public education and enlarge its responsibility for the extent, character, and quality of educational offerings—including services of public libraries—it will probably not take over education as its exclusive function. Equalization of opportunity and general supervision will doubtless continue to be the role of the state for many years. Its grants for education will continue to increase.

GRANTS FOR GENERAL PURPOSES

As has been indicated, the specific grants and payments of the federal government to the states and those of the states to the localities have been made for functions and purposes selected by the grantors in the furtherance of interests deemed important to them. These grants may have "stimulated" local governments to expand certain functions or may have caused them to levy taxes upon themselves (for matching) in order to support activities that but for the "free funds" they would not have undertaken. Quite apart from the social utility of the stimulated activities, funds may have been diverted from uses of equal or greater importance to citizens of some localities. It is too much to expect the federal government to cease imposing conditions on its grants or to refrain from designating the activities to be subsidized. Nor is it likely that the states may be induced to abandon all of their particular specifications. Lobby interests are too powerful in our central governments to permit this. Nevertheless, some of the stipulations might be relaxed and certainly many allocation formulas can be improved. The special grants, like special-purpose taxes, provide little help to "the general fund." They often produce an unbalance in funds available for public services. For example, school and library buildings may be more urgently needed than streets or highways. Funds, conditional on intergovernmental payments, may be available for one purpose leaving little or nothing for more urgent needs. This has led to the advocacy and timid development of grants for general purposes. The English block-grant system is of this type. There the maintenance of a given standard of local services frees grants-in-aid funds for general budgetary uses. The New York per capita grant system, which replaced the system of shared taxes, operates similarly.

In New York, cities and towns have received grants in proportion to population at specified per capita rates. These rates have been $6.75 for cities, $3.55 for towns, and $3.00 for villages.[28] Most grants in New York have been for specified purposes—educational equalization, transportation of pupils, school construction, teacher training, community colleges, school lunches and milk, highways, snow removal, public welfare, health services, housing subsidies, care of juvenile delinquents, civil defense, airport construction, and so on.[29] The per capita grants thus supplemented the traditional specific grants but were available for general purposes. The differentiation by cities, towns, and villages was chosen "for its close correlation with the needs of our municipalities"[30] and reflected differences in the

costs of providing services in the three types of government.[31]

Grants of this type and other intergovernmental transfers to general funds are of interest to all agencies and branches of government whose services are not subsidized by particular and specified payments. They augment the general funds of local governments and may be appropriated by budgeting authorities for such uses as are deemed important to them. Anything that increases the general funds thus makes available greater total resources to the various claimants. Unrestricted grants increase the authority of local appropriating agencies as to the use of funds. Typical grants, on the other hand, leave the decisions to Congress or state legislatures. It must be noted, however, that regardless of local desires for free funds, unconditional grants are few and do not seem to be increasing. However, as urban communities develop, as new satellites grow around more and more cities, as the standards of local services improve—or even become traditional —such grants may and should increase. Legislative redistricting may also lead

---

[28] Cf. *1957 Census of Governments, State Payments to Local Governments*, IV, No. 2, 62.

[29] *Ibid.*, pp. 62–64.

[30] *Report of the Commission on Municipal Revenues and Reduction of Real Estate Taxes* (New York, 1946), p. 19 ("Moore Commission").

[31] But note: "There are over sixty state-aid programs in New York State in addition to the famous per capita grant which was introduced in 1946. Special attention has been directed to a reconsideration of the role of the per capita grant at the local level which was substituted for revenues lost through the abolition of shared taxes. It was not justified by any systematic analysis of the relative needs of the communities. The per capita formula has remained fixed during the post-World War II period of changing local needs. Therefore, whatever fortuitous merit it might have had then (because for most communities it approximated the shared-tax revenues which were received) has been altered. It is hoped that by proper analysis the system of state aid may be simplified and that a fuller recognition may be given to the underlying needs and fiscal capacities of the local governments" (J. J. Carroll and S. Sacks, "Local Sources of Local Revenue," *Proceedings of the National Tax Association* [1961], pp. 294–95).

to greater consideration of the problems of urban governments—a matter of great concern to public libraries as well as other important services dependent upon the adequacy of local revenues.

CONCLUSION

This survey of local revenues confirms the fact that the general property tax continues to be the main support of local government in the United States. It is an institution. It continues to be inequitable. Such oversight and administrative supervision as the state has given have improved it very little. It was a defective tax from the very beginning and doubtless will continue that way. So long as income flows to citizens the property tax will collect substantial revenues from property owners. It may be improved somewhat by better state supervision.

The most important event affecting the course of local government revenues has been the increase in intergovernmental payments, or transfers, over the last fifty years. Grants-in-aid, of course, are older than that, but their fiscal importance is of comparatively recent origin. Nearly all intergovernmental payments are in aid of specific services selected by the grantors and are available under specific conditions to be met by the grantees. Federal payments have been made largely on the "stimulation" principle, necessitating matching payments for designated uses by state or local units. State grants have been more to equalize opportunities for local citizens, or to offset the fortuitous and differential distribution of taxable capacity among local governments. Educational grants and payments rank first among these transfers; public welfare grants are now more important than those for highways. Federal grants in small amounts are available for rural libraries. About a dozen states provide quite limited grants for local public libraries. Are these grants the beginning of more liberal financial aid to public libraries?

The further growth of intergovernmental payments to local governments may be expected and should be encouraged. It is especially important that the specific services to be encouraged be generalized, that distribution formulas be overhauled, and that such funds be made increasingly available to the general operating funds of local governments. They can then be appropriated according to local needs and local standards of public service instead of being used exclusively, as specified by general law (often at the behest of pressure groups). The warping of local services in order to secure available grants has been all too frequent under the present system. Unrestricted funds available for general budgetary use are a common need vouchsafed by many local officials. So far few intergovernmental payments meet this need. The English block grants and the limited per capita grants of New York are about the only examples.

The derivation of revenues by way of intergovernmental transfers is almost the only way in which local governments can secure the benefit of an equitable, well-balanced tax system. Such taxes require centralized administration and large territorial jurisdiction if they are to be effective in reaching the taxable capacity of citizens, business, and movable property owned by them. Those units best able to administer taxes should perform this work; those units best able to perform given services should be given that responsibility.

Funds should flow from those who can best collect revenues to those units that best can serve. This is not an easy situation to arrange, but at least the increasing importance of intergovernmental revenues indicates what is happening in a somewhat haphazard way. Further improvement is possible but will take years to accomplish.

Of course, this is not the only thing to work at in the improvement of the local revenue system. Every revenue device should be as effectively administered as possible. Indeed tax administration requires much knowledge as well as many specialized skills. The purchase of such competence is beyond the grasp of many of the smaller local units. Here, too, co-operation of the state and co-operative joint ventures of several municipalities would be profitable. A careful look at some of the minor sources of revenue is also desirable. Many of these produce far less revenue than they should, since many of the rates, fees, and prices have not been adjusted to keep pace with prices generally, or even with rising costs. Even so, these minor sources of income will not produce much revenue in the total for typical communities, but every bit will help.

Whatever improves the financial position of local governments is of great moment to public libraries. Their welfare is tied directly to the revenue systems of the governments that support them. The adequacy of those systems should be their major concern.

Finally, I hope I may be permitted one gratuitous and personal observation. If the libraries are interested in the revenues that support them, those who collect and publish library statistics should pay more attention to the sources and amounts of various library revenues. *The American Library Directory* gives one figure for the income of each library plus an amount spent for books (sometimes for periodicals, binding, and enrolment) and generally for salaries. It gives no detail whatever on income from taxes, library earnings, gifts, or endowment income (usually lacking). Such information would be a start. *The Library Statistics,* published by the Office of Education of the United States Department of Health, Education, and Welfare, present data on population served, staff, beginning salaries for library-school graduates, book stock, circulation, operating expenditures (by total, plus salaries, library materials, binding, and other costs), but not one column is devoted to library income or its components. It is time income data were collected and published! What would you think of a government statistics office that published data only on where the money went and completely ignored the basis and sources of support? Not only are revenue statistics needed but considerable research into sources of library income would be worthwhile. Not only would we learn more about the subject for its own sake, but what was discovered might help improve the position of the public library as a part of the local government structure and as one of the vital partners in public education.

CHARACTERISTICS OF THE MEDIUM-SIZED PUBLIC LIBRARY[1]

HOWARD W. WINGER

LIKE so many things important in American life, the medium-sized public library is a dream and an abstraction. It is no particular library, but it comprises the common characteristics of many particular libraries. The task of this paper is to define those characteristics that will serve as a basis for the ensuing discussions of this familiar institution.

The most obvious characteristic is the one of size. There are large libraries and small libraries. The medium-sized library falls between them. This shocking redundancy is presented to emphasize the quantitative nature of the definition. Medium-sized is not equated with mediocrity. A medium-sized public library may render distinguished service to the community.

The size of the library, which is so important in the definition, can best be put in terms of the number of people it serves. This measure of size is most convenient because it falls in line with the majority of statistical reports on public library service. A range of 25,000 to 150,000 population served has been chosen to define the medium-sized public library for this conference. The choice of the limits of this range has been affected by professional thought on the minimum feasible size of a public library to provide adequate library service. Only twenty years ago, that was considered to be 25,000 people.[2] By

1956 this minimum figure had been raised to include 100,000 to 200,000 people.[3] The upper figure of 150,000 people for the definition of the medium-sized public library falls at mid-range of the 1956 pronouncement. Logical or not, this choice of range raised some difficulties when it came to preparing papers about medium-sized public libraries. Statistical reports about libraries and communities vary in respect to the sizes of communities concerned. So dependent is social analysis on statistical sources that, in consequence of this variation, various authors have based their papers on slightly different ranges of population. The lack of current detailed reports on public libraries serving from 25,000 to 35,000 people, for example, almost eliminates libraries in that class from this report.

Besides the size of population served, one additional factor was taken into account in defining the medium-sized public library. As considered in this conference, the medium-sized public library is a locally autonomous unit serving a single community. Such units have been selected from the Library Services Branch reports covering the fiscal year 1960 by choosing those libraries not

---

[1] The tables were compiled with the assistance of Miss Elizabeth Fiss, student in the Graduate Library School, University of Chicago.

[2] American Library Association, Committee on Post-War Planning, *Post-War Standards for Public Libraries* (Chicago: American Library Association, 1942), p. 35.

[3] American Library Association, Co-ordinating Committee on the Revision of Public Library Standards, *Public Library Service in America: A Guide to Evaluation with Minimum Standards* (Chicago: American Library Association, 1956), p. 18.

labeled as giving county or regional service.

The following analysis, then, is based largely on 315 locally autonomous public libraries serving from 35,000 to 150,000 people. In this population range, there are an additional 344 libraries giving county or regional service. This total of 659 libraries is used in some of the tables for purposes of comparison. The 318 public libraries serving from 25,000 to 35,000 people are omitted from most of the discussion for lack of available data about them.

TABLE 1

NUMBER OF PUBLIC SCHOOL DISTRICTS IN THE UNITED STATES, 1942–57

Year	No. of Districts
1942	108,579
1951	70,452
1954	67,346
1957	50,446

STANDARDS FOR COMPARISON

The medium-sized public library can best be understood when related to two other things. First, it is a responsibility of the local government, and it needs to be placed in perspective with the other responsibilities of the local government. This is particularly pertinent in respect to local finances. Second, its performance as a library can be compared with the standards which librarians have established to measure performance as in the public library standards of 1956.

The comparison of the performance of the medium-sized public library with the standards of public library service set forth in 1956 is not altogether pertinent. Those standards for the most part ignored libraries serving fewer than 100,000 people. The use of the 1956 standards seems justifiable, however, for several reasons: (1) They are the only national standards, and it seems useful to ask how an important group of libraries left outside their scope compare with them. (2) Some of the libraries under discussion, those serving from 100,000 to 150,000 people, are large enough to stand comparison. (3) The 1956 standards were not based *arbitrarily* on a population of 100,000. This statement of minimum size was compounded of three elements: (*a*) a concept of essential services; (*b*) a consideration of the cost of such services; and (*c*) an estimate of the population necessary to sustain such costs. Even though the medium-sized libraries cannot be expected to measure up, the question is: How far do they come?

A LOCAL UNIT AND RESPONSIBILITY

In 1950, Robert D. Leigh reported for the Public Library Inquiry that the public library was a local unit and responsibility, locally initiated, financed, and controlled.[4] More than half the 6,700 public libraries then in the United States served populations of less than 5,000. In 1960, the number of public libraries had increased to 8,190 and still more than half of them served populations of less than 5,000. Bear in mind that these are autonomous administrative units—not branches or depots of larger systems—and the persistence of localism in public library development is clearly shown.

The contrast between library development and public school development in this respect is quite striking. In the same period of time, school districts (comparable administrative units to the autonomous libraries) have been growing larger and fewer (Table 1).

[4] *The Public Library in the United States* (New York: Columbia University Press, 1950), p. 56.

The steady trend toward the consolidation of school districts undoubtedly owes much to state leadership armed with state financial aid to public schools. However, despite the traditions of localism, public libraries serving populations between 35,000 and 150,000 also display a surprising amount of consolidation. In Table 2 we see the total number of libraries serving that population range paired with the number of libraries that are autonomous local units. This reveals that over half the libraries provide county or regional service. Some regional analysis, not shown in the table, demonstrates that regionalism is farthest advanced in the Southeast, where about 80 per cent of all libraries in our size range are regional or county systems. Perhaps the chief stronghold of library localism is in the Great Lakes and Plains region, where the *average* public library serves 16,000 people as compared to 34,000 people in the Southeast.[5]

FINANCIAL SUPPORT

The financial dependence of the public library on the local government restricts it to the kind of tax and tax base available for local functions. In most cases, this lays heavy responsibility on the general property tax. The yield of the tax depends on the rate levied and on the amount of assessed evaluation of property. The value of property in a community, in addition to the rate of tax the voters are willing to pay, becomes a key factor in the support of library services. A community which has industry may be in a fairly strong position because of the value of indus-

[5] United States Office of Education, Library Services Branch, *Statistics of Public Libraries Serving Populations of 100,000 or More* (OE-15033; Washington, D.C.: Government Printing Office, November, 1961), p. 4.

trial property. Homeowners in purely residential communities, on the other hand, have to absorb the whole burden. This heavier bill is a premium some homeowners have to pay to escape the smoke and crowding of an industrial center; but such a restricted local tax base increases the difficulty of securing adequate tax revenue to support local functions.

The homeowner, who is also a voter, has a firmer control over the amount of his property tax than he has over most taxes. Very often, proposals to increase

TABLE 2

MEDIUM-SIZED PUBLIC LIBRARIES IN
THE UNITED STATES, 1960

POPULATION OF COMMUNITY SERVED	TOTAL No. OF LIBRARIES	LOCAL UNITS	
		No.	Per Cent
25,000– 34,999	318	.....	.....
35,000– 49,999	250	124	49
50,000– 99,999	318	152	47
100,000–150,000	91	39	43

local rates or add new ones require public approval in tax referendums. This procedure provides the voter a much more direct control over his property taxes than he has over the income tax, the sales tax, or others levied by higher levels of government.

Library services, at least on the level they are commonly offered, do not cost very much. In my home village, for example, which has taxed itself at the maximum rate, an average home assessed at $7,500 pays $11.32 a year for library service: $7.50 for operating expense and $3.82 for building bond issues. This amount can be (and often has been) compared to the cost of so many bottles of liquor and so many cartons of cigarettes. Put on a monthly rate, $11.32 a year looks trivial, and in the early days of a community's development it is possible to shame citizens into voting for cultural improvements with just such comparisons. However, as the total tax bill climbs, voters have second thoughts. They might not use cigarettes or liquor, or they might see no clear way to reducing or holding down their costs. But they can very easily vote against tax increases.

At all events, there is a practical as well as a legal limitation on local revenues, at least on how rapidly they can be increased. Various public boards tacitly recognize this in the way they space their tax and bond referendums. To run two together is to increase the risk of defeat for the less popular (and maybe the chance of success for the more popular). Decent intervals must elapse between elections. Referendums are seldom scheduled for the same month in which the voters receive their tax bills.

In such circumstances, public agencies often seek reinforcement from each other. Libraries, for example, are tempted to solicit support from the schools because of library contributions to education. In view of the high juvenile circulation in public libraries, this seems like a natural argument. However, it is a dangerous argument for both the public library and the school. It may lead voters to denying to the schools the school libraries which they need on the grounds they have already supported a public library. The public library undoubtedly has a role in serving youth, but it cannot possibly substitute for libraries and librarians in every school. Besides, in addition to services to youth, the public library is responsible for providing services to adults.

Per capita support of public libraries. —The amount per capita which a community spends annually on the operating expense of a public library has been used as a standard of library service. In 1942, the annual expenditure of $1.00 per capita was thought sufficient for minimum service. The 1956 public library standards committee, feeling the impact of inflation and at the same time holding a more elevated view of the nature of adequate library service, did not propose an invariable standard of per capita support. Nevertheless, the principle was not abandoned. The committee drew up four illustrative budgets for the implementation of the standards, and these were revised in 1959 to account for cost of living increases.[6] From those 1959 budgets, per capita support figures can be derived. The budget for a community of 50,000 implied annual per capita support of $3.96 under 1959 conditions. For two communities of 100,000 each, allowing for some variable demands of service, per capita figures were $3.44 and $3.49. For one community of 135,000, the figure was $3.05.

These budgets, suggested for 1959 conditions, assumed that a beginning librarian could be hired for an annual salary of $4,600. According to a recent report, beginning professional librarians in 1961 could expect salaries ranging from $5,000 to $5,300.[7] Because the illustrative budgets allocated around 68 per cent for salaries, this item alone would call for upward revision of the per capita support figure in 1962.

Table 3 shows the average per capita support enjoyed by the 659 libraries (including the county and regional sys-

---

[6] American Library Association, Public Libraries Division, *Costs of Public Library Service in 1959* (Chicago: American Library Association, 1960).

[7] D. E. and R. B. Strout, "The Story Is the Same," *Library Journal*, LXXXVII (June 15, 1962), 2323.

tems) serving populations from 35,000 to 150,000 in 1960. None of the averages is equal to half the figure proposed in the 1959 budgets. When the 315 locally autonomous units are averaged alone, as in Table 3, average per capita support is higher, equaling half or two-thirds the standard. This is not enough, but it shows that on the average the local units are stronger than the average of county and regional systems. Obviously, combination into systems alone will not bring strong library service.

Per capita support and the special rate.—In some states, as in Illinois, library support depends on a special tax rate with a legal maximum. My experience with this law led me to wonder whether the low level of per capita support results from too low a maximum rate. Are libraries receiving the maximum rate and still deficient in income?

Illinois library statistics provide an answer to this question in respect to that particular state. They give the amount of total income, the amount of tax income, the amount of assessed evaluation, and the tax rate levied for each library. Table 4 presents this information for the Illinois public libraries. It shows the libraries with the median income in three population ranges in 1960. The per capita expenditures are respectively $2.02, $1.86, and $1.84. This level of support is far below that suggested in the budgets of 1959. Yet none of the libraries was taxing at so much as four-tenths the maximum legal rate. The maximum rate could increase the tax revenue for those libraries more than two-and-a-half times. A modest $3.50 to $4.00 per capita a year for library operation is within the reach of

TABLE 3

PER CAPITA SUPPORT FOR MEDIUM-SIZED AND
LOCAL-UNIT PUBLIC LIBRARIES, 1960

Range of Population Served	No. of Libraries	Average Per Capita Support	Average Total Expenditures
Medium-sized libraries:			
35,000– 49,999.....	250	$1.85	$ 59,000
50,000– 99,999.....	318	1.43	97,000
100,000–150,000.....	91	1.36	177,000
Local-unit libraries:			
35,000– 49,999.....	124	1.98	81,000
50,000– 99,999.....	152	2.06	153,000
100,000–150,000.....	39	2.10	239,000

TABLE 4

SUPPORT OF ILLINOIS PUBLIC LIBRARIES WITH MEDIAN INCOME, 1960

MEASURES AND FACTORS OF SUPPORT	POPULATION RANGE		
	25,000–34,999	35,000–49,999	50,000–99,999
Total income..............	$ 56,387	$ 79,730	$123,374
Tax income...............	$ 48,986	$ 68,018	$104,256
Population...............	27,878	43,047	66,780
Per capita support..........	$ 2.02	$ 1.86	$ 1.84
Assessed evaluation ($1000)..	$ 83,811	$100,936	$177,710
Tax rate (cents per $100 assessed evaluation)........	$ 0.062	$ 0.079	$ 0.066
Tax income available at maximum rate of .20..........	$167,622	$201,872	$355,420
No. of libraries.............	16*	9	12†

* Ninth ranking from top used as median.
† Seventh ranking from top used as median.

these communities. The failure to provide it lies not so much in the tax law as in the failure of the communities to vote the necessary rate.

LIBRARY SERVICES

In his study of the optimum size of the public library unit, Lowell Martin set forth three essentials of service: (1) The book collection should provide "the basic and important books of our time about common personal and social problems." (2) There should be "personal assistance by experienced librarians in such specialized areas as children's

TABLE 5

Average Number of Volumes in Book Collections and Average Number of Volumes Added in 1960 for 315 Medium-Sized Libraries

Range of Population Served	No. of Libraries	Average No. of Volumes in Collection	Average No. of Volumes Added
35,000– 49,999.....	124	69,000	4,500
50,000– 99,999.....	152	107,000	7,300
100,000–150,000.....	39	170,000	12,300

reading, adult reading, and 'specialized cataloging and book-organizing skill.'" (3) "Minimum public service provides an organization of materials that facilitates and guides their use for popular educational purposes."[8] These statements of essentials are somewhat vague, but some specific measures of the book collection and of the amount of personal assistance a library should offer were set forth in the public library standards of 1956. It is possible to compare the performance of the medium-sized public libraries with those measures.

[8] Lowell Martin, "The Optimum Size of the Public Library Unit," *Library Extension: Problems and Solutions,* ed. C. B. Joeckel (Chicago: University of Chicago Press, 1946), pp. 38–39.

BOOK COLLECTIONS

The national standards for public libraries serving communities of 100,000 people prescribed a collection of 100,000 currently useful volumes and yearly additions of 4,000 to 5,000 separate titles, of which 400 to 500 were to be children's titles and 250 were to be new adult titles of interest to young adults. This standard is only partly quantitative, and a general statistical application of it meets with difficulties. Libraries report the number of volumes in their collections, but not whether they are "currently useful." They report the number of *volumes* added each year, but not the number of *titles*—much less the public for which the new volumes are intended. However, these gross measures provide a clue to a library's performance.

As shown in Table 5, the size of the book collection and the annual rate of book acquisition would seem to be one of the strongest points of the medium-sized public library. The average library serving from 100,000 to 150,000 people seems to meet the standard in all sections of the country—something which cannot be said of the measures of per capita support, or (as will be seen later) the standard of adequate staffing. In the Northeast and Midwest, the average libraries serving only from 50,000 to 100,000 people were strong enough to bring the national average up to the minimum standards. Although the average library serving from 35,000 to 50,000 people could not meet the standard set for communities two to three times as large, it went far more than halfway toward it. These averages are for the locally autonomous libraries, however, and the inclusion of county and regional systems would yield reduced figures.

LIBRARY CIRCULATION

Annual circulation is a measure of the use of a book collection. In 1960, the annual aggregate circulation of all public libraries serving over 35,000 population exceeded 454,000,000 volumes (Table 6). Although some libraries reported only their total circulation, most libraries classified the circulation according to juvenile and adult materials. In the classified reports, juvenile circulation equaled nearly 204,000,000 volumes, while adult circulation was about 184,000,000. If unclassified circulation is to be distributed in a like ratio, 52 per cent of all items circulated from public libraries in the group are juvenile items.

Shown in Table 7 are average circulation figures for all public libraries serving from 35,000 to 100,000 people. When these average circulations are

TABLE 6

CIRCULATION OF PUBLIC LIBRARIES SERVING 35,000 OR MORE POPULATION, 1960

SIZE OF POPULA-TION SERVED	No. OF LI-BRARIES	CIRCULATION (THOUSANDS OF VOLUMES)		
		Total	Adult	Juvenile
35,000–49,999..	250	45,045	19,617	22,563
50,000–99,999..	318	93,178	38,027	47,510
Over 100,000....	254	316,483	126,657	133,529
Total........	822	454,706	184,301	203,602

compared with the average circulations of the locally autonomous libraries (Table 8), the familiar fact emerges that the local units are stronger. Another fact also emerges in the comparison of national averages for the two groups of libraries of smaller size. When the local units are considered alone, the average preponderance of juvenile circulation disappears. The evidence at hand does

not provide a reason for this, but one thinks of the regional library's familiar bookmobile wending its way through the country and making its stops at the schools. The reappearance of the juvenile preponderance in libraries serving from 100,000 to 150,000 population is another puzzling factor. Is this traceable to the greater prevalence of neighborhood branches in the larger communities? A select list of 106 libraries

TABLE 7

AVERAGE CIRCULATION OF PUBLIC LIBRARIES SERVING 35,000 OR MORE PEOPLE, 1960

RANGE OF POPULATION SERVED	AVERAGE CIRCULATION (THOUSANDS OF VOLUMES)		
	Total	Adult	Juvenile
35,000–49,999....	180	78	90
50,000–99,999....	291	119	148

(compiled by taking every fifth library in each state from those autonomous units serving 100,000 to 150,000 people) shows that they average 3.4 branches per library compared to 1.4 and 0.5 for select lists of the successively smaller units. It is also true, as will be shown later, that the larger libraries are better supplied with children's librarians than those of the two smaller groups.

Regional analysis locates the great preponderance of juvenile circulation in the Great Lakes and Plains region. In two other regions of the country adult circulation is consistently higher, and in the third it varies. This may be related to the differing arrangements libraries have with the schools. The difference such arrangements can make in circulation is illustrated by two Indiana cities in the 100,000–150,000 class. The Public Library of Hammond, Indiana, which gives service to the schools, circulated over 1,200,000 volumes, of which nearly three-fourths (over 880,-000) were classified as juvenile. The Public Library of South Bend, Indiana, which does not report special service to the schools, had 926,000 circulation in 1960, of which 464,000 (only slightly more than half) was juvenile. When this factor is taken into account for all thirty-nine local-unit libraries serving

books, the amount of public library effort spent in serving juveniles is even more impressive.

THE LIBRARIANS

The second minimum essential of library service calls for a specialized staff. The illustrative budgets proposed to implement the 1956 public library standards included personnel tables providing for specialized staffs. These

TABLE 8

AVERAGE CIRCULATION OF 315 LOCAL-UNIT LIBRARIES, 1960

(Thousands of Volumes)

RANGE OF POPULATION SERVED	CIRCULATION BY REGION				
	North Atlantic	Great Lakes and Plains	West and Southwest	Southeast	National
35,000–49,999:					
Total..........	198	291	220	111	219
Adult..........	106	130	115	57	109
Juvenile........	91	161	97	62	109
50,000–99,999:					
Total..........	388	384	312	214	348
Adult..........	197	171	184	113	175
Juvenile........	191	213	126	100	173
100,000–150,000:					
Total..........	429	700	779	347	604
Adult..........	228	283	419	162	287
Juvenile........	201	417	359	185	317

populations from 100,000 to 150,000, we find that seven of fourteen libraries in the Great Lakes and Plains region provide school service, but only one of nine in the North Atlantic, only three of ten in the West and Southwest, and only one of six in the Southeast.

Despite differences in organization, size, and region, however, juvenile circulation is impressively high in the medium sized public library everywhere in the United States. About half of all the books that go out of the library are juvenile books. Since juveniles are fewer in number than adults and they often take out advanced as well as juvenile

tables called for librarians who have specialized in reference, adult services, extension, cataloging, work with children and young people, bookmobile work, audio-visual materials, and administration. The number of professional and clerical workers suggested in the budgets ran from fourteen professionals and fifteen clerks in the smallest library budgeted to thirty-four professionals and fifty-two clerks in the largest. The comparative figures for the different budgets are shown in Table 9.

Although the personnel tables were proposed for libraries of particular sizes with particular tasks, they were put forth as being illustrative of the staffs necessary to provide adequate library service. Table 10 shows the actual personnel complements of the average libraries serving the three different ranges of population under consideration. As to be expected, the number of positions filled in libraries serving from 35,000 to 50,000 is on the average far below the standards. Nor are larger libraries, on the average, up to standards. The average library in the North Atlantic region serving from 50,000 to 100,000 people almost meets standards for a library serving 50,000 people, but the average library in no other region does. Only in the West and Southwest does the average library serving from 100,000 to 150,000 people meet standards for libraries serving 100,000 people, but it does not equal that for 135,-000 people.

The small average figure for professional positions vacant may cause some librarians to raise an eyebrow. The Library Services Branch states: "These vacancy figures do not reflect a complete picture of professional staff shortages; because of the scarcity of trained personnel, some positions are filled temporarily by employees with less than adequate qualifications."[9]

What are professional qualifications? If a degree from an accredited library school is required to qualify for a professional position, the medium-sized public library is likely to go long understaffed. In 1961, only 387 graduates of accredited library schools took positions in public libraries of all sizes and descriptions.[10] The 315 public libraries in our special scope had (according to averages) more than 387 vacancies in

[9] United States Office of Education, *op. cit.*, p. 20.

[10] Strout, *op. cit.*, p. 2327.

1960. Add to these the number of vacancies in larger and smaller libraries and in county and regional systems and the personnel shortage becomes more impressive. Add to that figure the number of professional librarians required to bring libraries up to standard and the number becomes spectacular!

CURRENT SPECIALIZATION IN LIBRARY STAFFS

To get a closer look at library staffs at work in the 315 libraries, a sample of 106 libraries was secured by selecting

TABLE 9

NUMBER OF FULL-TIME PROFESSIONAL AND CLERICAL POSITIONS SUGGESTED IN FOUR ILLUSTRATIVE BUDGETS FOR LIBRARIES TO MEET STANDARDS OF SERVICE

Type of Worker	Budget I (50,000 People)	Budget II (100,000 People)	Budget III (100,000 People)	Budget IV (135,000 People)
Professional.	14	21	21	34
Clerical.....	15	30	30	52
Total....	29	51	51	86

from the total list every fifth library from each state. The result is a third rather than a fifth of the total number, and some states are overrepresented because libraries do not come in groups of five. However, because library development proceeds under state laws which vary from state to state, it is important to have each commonwealth represented.

First, let us take a look at the head librarian. There is an impression that the librarian of the medium-sized public library is a woman. This is true only of some libraries. Reference to the latest *American Library Directory* (New York: R. R. Bowker Company, 1962) reveals that 60 of the 106 head librarians are women, but 46 are men. The men had a better chance in the larger libraries. In 21 libraries serving from 100,000 to 150,000 population, the men outnumbered the women 15 to 6. In the smaller libraries, however, the women outnumbered the men 54 to 31.

Unfortunately, this same source did not reveal more pertinent characteristics such as the education and other professional qualifications of the head li-

esses third. Other kinds of professional specializations are widely scattered. As to be expected, the libraries serving more than 100,000 people are able to supply more specialized personal assistance than the smaller ones. They averaged at least a cataloger, a reference librarian, and a children's librarian each. They were also more likely to have a subject specialist.

TABLE 10

AVERAGE NUMBER OF POSITIONS FILLED IN LOCALLY AUTONOMOUS
PUBLIC LIBRARIES SERVING POPULATIONS FROM 35,000
TO 150,000 IN 1960

REGION AND SIZE OF POPULATION SERVED	EQUIVALENT OF FULL-TIME POSITIONS			
	No. of Positions Filled			Professional Positions Vacant
	Total	Clerical	Profes-sional	
35,000–49,999:				
North Atlantic........	16.6	8.6	8.0	1.4
Great Lakes and Plains.	16.6	11.4	5.2	1.1
West and Southwest....	11.5	7.4	4.1	1.0
Southeast.............	8.1	5.8	2.3	1.0
50,000–99,999:				
North Atlantic........	32.3	20.3	12.0	0.4
Great Lakes and Plains.	27.0	18.9	8.1	1.2
West and Southwest....	19.9	13.2	6.7	0.8
Southeast.............	12.8	9.9	2.9	1.5
100,000–150,000:				
North Atlantic........	40.2	24.1	16.1	1.5
Great Lakes and Plains.	48.7	35.2	13.5	1.6
West and Southwest....	59.3	38.8	20.5	1.2
Southeast.............	26.0	20.0	6.0	1.1

brarian. Nor does it yield that information about the other specialized librarians listed with their libraries. However, the directory includes names of the reference librarians, children's librarians, etc., and this information indicates the range and frequency of specializations in medium-sized public libraries (Table 11).

The most frequently occurring specialization is reference work, followed by work with children and young people, with cataloging and technical proc-

We cannot infer much more from this source. It is not clear whether all specialists were listed, or whether only responsible heads of departments were included. But the report gives a glimpse at the range of specialization.

OTHER ESSENTIALS OF SERVICE

The third minimum essential of library service is "an organization of materials that facilitates and guides their use for popular educational purposes." The meeting of this requirement is the function of the book collections and the staffs already discussed, and I cannot add much to it from my sources.

A fourth essential, mentioned but slighted by Martin in his paper on the optimum size of the library, is the library building. Unfortunately, no agency publishes systematic information about library buildings. Librarians write sporadically to library periodicals about their new buildings, but the re-

perience is cited only to show that the board had to gather its own evidence and that there is a need for systematic reporting on library buildings.

CONCLUSION

In presenting the characteristics of the medium-sized public library, it has been held up to the not entirely appropriate standards proposed in 1956 for units serving 100,000 or more people.

TABLE 11

SPECIALIZED POSITIONS IN 106 SELECTED MEDIUM-SIZED PUBLIC LIBRARIES

SPECIALIZATION	FREQUENCY OF SPECIALIZATION, BY SIZE OF POPULATION SERVED		
	35,000–49,999	50,000–99,999	100,000–150,000
Assistant or associate librarian	7	10	4
Reference, interlibrary loan........	21	37	22
Children and young adult.........	16	27	22
Circulation.....................	5	12	12
Cataloging, technical processes.....	11	21	20
Adult services, readers' adviser.....	5	4	5
Subject specialists...............	3	3	11
Extension......................	0	1	8
Schools.......................	0	2	3
Miscellaneous*..................	2	7	10
Total no. of libraries...........	42	43	21
Average no. of specialized positions......................	1.6	3.0	5.5

* Hospital, audio-visual, bibliographer, administrative assistant, branch, popular reading.

ports are not consistent or uniform. To locate information even on famous new public library buildings is difficult after the dedicating splurge has passed. Two years ago when the Board of Directors of the Park Forest (Illinois) Public Library proposed a bond issue to enlarge the building, the librarian gathered comparative statistics about library buildings in nearby communities. A major purpose of this collection of facts was to demonstrate the need for space by pointing to other libraries which had more, and there is not much of general value in the figures. The ex-

Although we have defined the medium-sized public library as one serving from 25,000 to 150,000 people, there are no national standards for the smaller libraries in this group. There are not even nationally gathered and published reports for libraries serving less than 35,000 people, nor have such reports been announced for inclusion in the Library Services Branch statistical series.

It is not surprising to find that the average library serving fewer than 50,-000 people fails to meet the standards. The average library serving 50,000 to 100,000 people meets the standards for book collections and acquisitions, judging from gross figures reported, but is below standards in personnel. The average library in the group serving 100,000 to 150,000 people has a much stronger book collection and acquisitions program, but it is also greatly understaffed except in the West and Southwest region. The average library in every group is far below the standard of annual per capita support.

A suggested remedy for substandard libraries is combination into larger units. Inasmuch as performance depends on logically derived standards of financial support, combination into systems alone will not bring the locally autonomous medium-sized public library up to standards. Indeed, county and regional systems now existing to serve equivalent populations are on the average weaker than the local units. Combination must be accompanied by increased revenue to supply adequate service.

If different medium-sized public libraries serving contiguous territories were to unite to bring their aggregate populations to the base of 100,000, they could perhaps benefit from united collections and from a better distribution of specialized personnel. However, statistical averages make it appear that combination has more frequently occurred with much weaker local units than those which have served for the basis of this survey. Such combinations fill in the area on the map which shows communities receiving library service, but the level of service must be low.

The persistence of the small and medium-sized, locally autonomous units indicates there may be serious obstacles to union, that there may be advantages to localism, or both. Certainly obstacles to union exist, rooted in the tradition of

the public library as a locally initiated and supported institution. In Illinois, at least, the formation of each library district that crosses boundaries of local governments requires a campaign for confederation. This requires the approval of voters in every local unit involved. Such unanimous approval presents a political hurdle. In southern Cook County, for example, where many libraries serving contiguous territories could profit from a union, a proposal to combine faces not only the problems of differing tax rates and forms of government, but it also finds an area where some villages that have celebrated their centennials are unequally yoked with rapidly developing postwar suburbs. Differing concepts of local loyalty stemming from this pose a not inconsiderable barrier. To avoid civil war, perhaps, the Illinois law for union also guarantees the right of secession.

If there are obstacles to union, there may also be advantages to localism. This very local control and responsibility which sometimes makes it hard to raise the needed funds for library development, in the broader view, has its advantages. People *ought* to exercise control and feel responsibility for public functions. If they have services, they *ought* to pay for them, and they *ought* to know what they are paying for and why. Such responsible democracy is most easily achieved on the local level of government. The only justification for moving away from the local unit to the larger system would be to make it possible to provide better service for the combining local units as well as extending service to new territories. The loss of any exercise in local *responsibility* through the process would be a disadvantage of the larger system.

Legal limitations on library revenue

do not seem so serious a handicap to adequate library financing as does the failure of communities to exercise legal means to support libraries. It should be possible for library leaders who believe in the value of public library service to secure public support for it. This need not be at the expense of other governmental services. Actually, though the argument is well worn now, people do spend money on things, non-governmental in nature, which are not so valuable to them as library service. They must, however, be convinced of their need by something stronger than a ritual comparison of books with cigarettes.

Besides financial support (and only partially connected with it), the next most consistent average deficiency of the medium-sized public library is its lack of enough personnel. Among the larger units surveyed, only the average library in the West and Southwest region meets personnel standards. Libraries serving smaller communities are below. Not enough qualified librarians are available in the country to bring these libraries up to the standard of personnel complement.

The shortage of librarians in these libraries means they cannot offer the specialized personal assistance that the standards propose. Without enough children's librarians, children will have to find their own way to the bookshelves. Without reference librarians, the inexpert user may have to explore on his own the informational resources of the library. Perhaps the circulation of books is the major service many of these libraries can offer. This is not a trivial service. For a child to go to the shelf and get a book to take home has value of its own. For an adult to follow his individual interests through a well-chosen book collection has a value of its own. It is only to be hoped in view of the shortage of librarians that the children's librarian will be busy selecting, organizing, and promoting books, rather than slipping them. It is to be hoped that the reference librarian will likewise be engaged in providing appropriate reference materials and making them easily available. Shortage of librarians calls for economy of their efforts.

Unthinking criticism of the contribution a public library makes to the community through the circulation of books is somewhat like the criticism leveled at Red Grange, the galloping halfback, because he did not block, tackle, pass, and punt with the same grace and ease he displayed in carrying a football across the goal line. When Coach Robert Zuppke heard that criticism he retorted, alluding to a concert star of the day: "All Galli Curci can do is sing!" The point is that the specialty was a basic one—and so is the public library's circulation of books. The popular collections and the open shelves which make this possible were won by the American public libraries in historic battles of the nineteenth century. It is this very feature that has fostered in so many the happy memories and the local loyalties that are an important part of the abstraction and the dream which is the medium-sized public library.

TRENDS IN JUVENILE AND YOUNG ADULT
USE AND SERVICES

FORREST L. MILLS

CHILDREN and young adults are among the heaviest users of the public library. It is impossible today to consider public library service to these age groups without attention to increases in school enrolment, changes in the school curriculum and methods of teaching, and weaknesses of the school library. These three factors largely explain the unprecedented use of public library facilities by children and young people of school age. One must agree with James E. Bryan, President of the American Library Association, when he stated: "The educational demands on libraries are growing more rapidly than the standards are being met."[1] Indeed, one cannot but suspect that the gap between present demand and present capacity will be narrowed or closed not simply by new co-operative arrangements between and among libraries, but that additional materials, facilities, and staff will be required before the problems can be solved.

The discussion that follows will consider in turn: (1) increases in population as reflected in expected school enrolment; (2) changes in the curriculum and methods of teaching; (3) changes in service patterns of use, circulation, acquisition, reference and information work, and programs in the medium-sized public library; and (4) the secondary school library.

SCHOOL ENROLMENT TRENDS

The high birth rate of the 1950's served to reduce the median age of the population in the United States from 30.2 years in 1950 to 29.5 in 1960.[2] This, of course, is reflected in increased school enrolments. Kindergarten and elementary-school enrolments increased 50 per cent from 1950 to 1960 and are expected to rise 30 per cent more in the next twenty years. As the 1950 infants advance in years, this expansion in the school population will be felt in the high schools. High-school enrolments, which increased 54 per cent in the last decade, are expected in the next twenty years to rise nearly 62 per cent more. College enrolments are expected to increase a staggering 235 per cent from 1960 to 1980![3]

Reflected in these figures of increasing enrolments is a trend toward lengthening the period of education for all. Our society, which during the two decades following World War I universalized secondary education, seems now intent on making the opportunity for a higher education also universal. In Wisconsin, for example, the trend is well under way. Enrolment in state-supported schools of higher education doubled during the ten years ending 1962; during the decade ending 1972, enrolment is expected to increase another 92 per cent.[4]

---

[1] "Mutual Responsibility for Mutual Service," *College and Research Libraries,* XXIII (July, 1962), 294.

[2] Frank L. Schick (ed.), "Future of Library Service: Demographic Aspects and Implications," *Library Trends,* X, No. 1 (July, 1961), 27.

[3] *Ibid.,* p. 59, Table 18.

[4] Gaylord Nelson, Address at Oshkosh State College, April 27, 1962, Table 4.

What do these increased enrolments mean for public libraries? Unless school (including elementary, secondary, and collegiate) libraries and public libraries develop more rapidly than they have during the past twenty years, these increases can only mean that things will get a lot worse before they get better. The medium-sized public library is today often operating very nearly to capacity in its physical facilities, staff, and material resources. Increases in school enrolments seem likely to place additional heavy burdens upon it.

CURRICULUM AND TEACHING METHODS

To the layman there appear to be three important changes which have taken place in the school curriculum during recent years: (1) There has been a realization that the curriculum revision, if it is to be successful, must result in changed behavior, not only on the part of the student but of the teacher as well. (2) In consequence of this, there has been a shift from the execution of curriculum revision by administrators and consultants to procedures that assure wide participation by teachers, often by laymen, and sometimes by students, with an emphasis on day-to-day co-operative planning by teachers and students. (3) The objectives of the curriculum have shifted from mastery of a technique, a skill, or a set body of knowledge to the identification and exploration of what some writers call "persistent life problems" in a social or group situation, encouraging the development of skills necessary for the individual to work successfully with others.

The effect of the shifts in the emphasis of the curriculum is indicated in writings on the subject. J. Minor Gwynn, in his textbook, *Curriculum*

Principles and Social Trends, writing of the elementary school, states:

. . . Some educators would go so far as to abandon entirely all scheduled class periods and the organization of the curriculum around subject-matter fields.

The chief characteristic of the modern organization of the curriculum, then, is the integration of learning matter into comprehensive units. The problem method, the project method, and other approaches have been advocated, the underlying idea of each being to organize the curriculum into meaningful areas of activity.[5]

Implied in the project and problem methods is a demand for more sources of information than the single textbook of many years ago. This need was set forth explicitly in Part II of the Fifty-sixth Yearbook of the National Society for the Study of Education:

Procedures leading to selective critical reading in social studies are premised upon children's having a number of books at their disposal. Extensive reading from many sources is one of the key characteristics of the emerging program. Intensive reading and rereading of a single textbook continues in wide use, but there are few who defend it as good practice. Neither from the standpoint of getting various views of the same topic nor from the standpoint of individual differences of the learners can the use of a single text be championed.[6]

When the textbook goes out, of course, the library, ready or not, must enter.

The implications of the new curriculum and methods for a medium-sized public library can be illustrated with an account of a core program in social studies planned for a tenth-grade class in a high school serving a city of 30,000 people. Among the topics included in the year's work in this core program

[5] 3d ed.; New York: Macmillan Co., 1960, pp. 199–200.

[6] *Social Studies in the Elementary School* (prepared by the Yearbook Committee, Ralph C. Preston, Chairman [Chicago: Distributed by the University of Chicago Press, 1957]), p. 196.

were these: (1) the development of the modern state; (2) natural resources and technological development in four countries being studied; (3) historical background of American participation in international affairs from colonial time onward; (4) American foreign policy in relation to the four nations; and (5) economic, political, and social aspects of nuclear energy.[7] Does the high-school library have resources to meet the demands of this course? Does the public library?

In *Focus on Change: Guide to Better Schools,* a report prepared for the Commission on the Experimental Study of Utilization of the Staff in the Secondary School, the director, J. Lloyd Trump, emphasizes certain points that, should the recommendations of the report be implemented, will be of great importance to all public libraries. In the words of Trump:

In the school of tomorrow students will undertake special projects which they have selected themselves or which teachers have suggested. The projects will clarify, add to, and enrich subject matter presented in large classes and further explored by discussion in small classes.[8]

The report envisions the future high-school week to comprise 30 hours, distributed as follows: 40 per cent of the time to be spent in large-group instruction involving perhaps 100–150 pupils; 20 per cent to be spent in small-group discussion involving up to fifteen pupils per group; and 40 per cent devoted to independent study.[9] These proposals,

of course, present a radical break with the organization that prevails today in many high schools. But they are not out of line with current trends.

Among other changes in public school practice that are exerting, and will continue to exert, an influence on the public library we may briefly note three: the development of special instructional programs for the gifted student; the growing emphasis on foreign language instruction in the middle, if not the early, grades; and the special attention given in some communities to students who are culturally disadvantaged. Programs for these children, whose failure in the first or early grades results largely from a lack of reading skill, may involve an all-day kindergarten session with exposure, through stories and field trips, to many of the experiences that the typical first-grader may already be familiar with: folklore, television, museums, parks, zoos, and nature walks.

PUBLIC LIBRARY USE BY CHILDREN AND YOUNG PEOPLE

Lack of uniform information makes changes in the use of the public library by children and young people difficult to describe. Statistics gathered by the Library Services Branch, although improved over previous years, provide little help in defining the dimensions of the public library service to children, to say nothing of service to young adults. The only direct measure of service reported distinguishes circulation to adults and to children. Reports on book collections no longer categorize adult and juvenile portions, nor do data on expenditures for books distinguish between adult and juvenile purchases. The report on adult-juvenile registration has evidently been discontinued.

[7] Florence B. Statemeyer *et al., Developing a Curriculum for Modern Living* (2d ed., rev. and enl.; New York: New York Teachers College, 1957), chap. xiii, esp. pp. 593 ff.

[8] J. L. Trump and D. Baynham, *Focus on Change: Guide to Better Schools* (Chicago: Rand McNally Co., 1961), p. 27.

[9] *Ibid.,* p. 41.

Because of the lack of consistently gathered information, everyone interested in this matter is looking forward to the publication of *A Guide to School/ Public Library Relations*. To be prepared by Mrs. D. R. Watts and Miss Elaine Simpson and published in the *Wilson Library Bulletin,* the guide is based on a comprehensive questionnaire relating to the use of public libraries by high-school students, organization and staffing of public libraries for services to young people, hours of service, staffing and book budgets in school libraries, and co-operation between schools and public libraries. With or without such data, however, no public librarian need be told that a marked increase in student use of public libraries is perhaps the major development of the past decade.

Every public librarian is acquainted with holiday jams created by students writing term papers. A survey conducted in the Newark (New Jersey) Public Library verifies the school-related nature of this rush. A questionnaire was filled out by 5,000 people of the 20,000 who came to the Main Library and Business Library, December 19–31, 1960. Of the respondents, over 64 per cent were students. Seventy per cent of all respondents had serious reference objectives. Forty-eight per cent were students working to complete school assignments and 22 per cent sought information relevant to trade or business concerns. Less than 25 per cent of the respondents visited the library for general informational or recreational reading.[10]

Generally, over 90 per cent of the public libraries serving more than 10,000 people provide reference service to children, high school students, and college students.[11] Surveys of specific libraries reveal how much of the total reference service goes to this class of user. In a two-day use survey (November and December, 1960) the Youngstown and Mahoning County (Ohio) Library reported that of nearly 1,000 persons using the main library adult reference service, 68 per cent were students.[12] A one-day patron count (April 19, 1961) made by Evansville (Indiana) Public Library, indicated that 63 per cent of 2,005 visitors to twelve library agencies were children and 12 per cent were young adults. Thus, 75 per cent of the total may be considered to be of school or college age.[13]

In 1961 the Committee on Student Use of the Library of the Los Angeles Public Library published the results of a month-long survey (March 9, 1959 to April 4, 1959), which showed that students using the branch facilities were distributed according to grade level in the following percentages: (1) elementary, 38.1; (2) senior high, 26.5; (3) junior high, 19.9; and (4) college and other post high school, 15.5.[14]

Stockton (California) Public Library made a six-day survey of use in January, 1959. Respondents included nearly five thousand children and adults.

[10] J. E. Bryan, "The Christmas Holiday Jam: Student Use of a Metropolitan Public Library," *ALA Bulletin,* LV (June, 1961), 526–30.

[11] American Library Association. Reference Services Division, "Reference Service in American Public Libraries Serving Populations of 10,000 or More," *University of Illinois Library School Occasional Papers,* LXI (March, 1961), 5.

[12] *Public Library Abstracts* (October, 1961), No. 61–479.

[13] *Evansville Staff News Bulletin,* June 1, 1961, pp. 61–73, par. 142.

[14] "Student Use of the Library: Report of Survey Conducted March 9, 1959–April 4, 1959," *Progress Report,* February, 1960, p. 1. (Hereinafter cited as "Student Use of the Library.")

Among the interesting findings were these: (1) Nearly 50 per cent of all library users were found to be pupils, teachers, or adult students; (2) 33 per cent of those using library materials used them for research purposes; (3) nearly one-third of the users were high-school graduates and over 20 per cent had attended college; and (4) 70 per cent of the respondents were under forty years of age.[15]

CIRCULATION

The most notable change over the past twenty years in the circulation pattern of public libraries has been the marked increase in the ratio of juvenile to total circulation—rising steadily from 33 per cent in 1939 to 50 per cent in 1954. Since 1954 this proportion has varied from 49 per cent to 51 per cent.[16] A survey of twenty-six public libraries whose service areas (1950 Census) included a population of 50,000–100,000 showed that in 1959 the proportion of juvenile to total circulation ranged from 25 per cent to 70 per cent, with the median at 50 per cent.[17]

There is at least one striking exception to the nationwide proportion of 50 per cent juvenile circulation. Howard Samuelson, Librarian of the Santa Ana Public Library, has gathered 1961 data on twenty-one California libraries, all but two of which may properly be considered as medium-sized. In 1961 the proportion of juvenile circulation ranged from 61.7 per cent to 25.5 per cent, with the median at 41 per cent, substantially less than the national figure.[18]

This decided difference between California libraries and those in the nation at large may be explained by availability to California children of good school-related library and book service through: (1) relatively well-established and well-supported school libraries in California; and (2) a provision of the state law that permits county libraries to manage and maintain school libraries. In 1956–57, for example, twenty-eight county libraries in California spent nearly 40 per cent of their materials budget for school purposes; over 40 per cent of the volumes added and over 35 per cent of the volumes owned were for school library service.[19]

Aside from factors discussed elsewhere, a partial explanation for the increase in the proportion of juvenile circulation may be found in the increase in mobile units—from 603 in 1950 to over 900 in 1956. During the same period the share of total circulation accounted for by bookmobiles increased by 60 per cent, that is, from 7 per cent of total circulation to 11.1 per cent.[20] In a survey of bookmobile service published in 1960, Mary Craig of the Fort Wayne and Allen County Public Library reported that only 7 per cent of the 357 libraries covered in the survey did not give bookmobile service to schools; 93 per cent served both school and non-school stops.[21] Twenty-seven

[15] Stockton and San Joaquin County Public Library, "Six-Day Library Usage Survey Conducted at Stockton Public Library and Its Two City Branches, January 12–17, 1959" (Stockton, Calif., 1959).

[16] ALA Bulletin, LV (July–August, 1961), 646.

[17] Unpublished data gathered by F. L. Mills.

[18] Unpublished data gathered by Howard Samuelson.

[19] California Public Library Commission, General Report (Berkeley, 1959), p. 62.

[20] United States Department of Health, Education and Welfare, Office of Education, Biennial Survey of Education in the United States—1954–56, chap. v: Statistics of Public Libraries: 1955–56 (Washington, D.C.: Government Printing Office, 1959), pp. 29–30.

[21] M. Craig, "Public Library Bookmobile Operation" (prepared by the staff of the Public Library of Fort Wayne and Allen County, Indiana, 1960), p. 7.

per cent of the respondents reported that their bookmobile service was designed predominantly for children. Many of the 73 per cent who replied that their bookmobile service was not planned mainly for children commented on the heavy use by children because their bookmobiles made school stops.[22]

BOOK COLLECTIONS

A survey completed several months ago by the Racine (Wisconsin) Public Library was concerned with title and volume acquisition in medium-sized public libraries (serving areas of 50,000–100,000 population, 1950 Census).[23] Twenty libraries responded, and fifteen supplied usable data concerning the acquisition of juvenile titles. In 1959 the median library added 691 juvenile titles, the range being from 1,868 to 504. The question was asked: "Considering the objectives of your library and its service area and without regard to funds available for book purchase, what should the approximate levels of annual book acquisition be?" Fifteen estimates were given for juvenile title acquisition. Two-thirds of the estimates ranged from 600 to 1,000 titles and one-third estimated 1,200 titles or more.

The survey found that in nine of the libraries juvenile title acquisition in 1959 was 33 per cent more than the five-year average for 1951–55. In eighteen libraries average juvenile volume acquisition was up 8.2 per cent. It seems reasonable to assume, therefore, that medium-sized public libraries today are buying considerably more juvenile titles than they bought five to ten years ago. In 1954, Racine, for example, added 361 juvenile titles and 4,271 volumes—

a title-volume ratio of 11.7. In 1961, the library added 967 titles and 7,254 volumes, a title-volume ratio of 7.4. This decided increase in acquisition has been occasioned, one suspects, less by a rise in the quality of literature produced for children than by the greatly enlarged dimensions of subject matter in elementary and junior high school curriculums, and in a correlative increase in juvenile titles produced. Of twenty-six libraries reporting, twenty-four spent more for books and periodicals in 1959 than they averaged for the five years 1951–55. Five reported increases ranging from 50 per cent to 99 per cent; four reported increases ranging from 100 per cent to 199 per cent; and one library reported an increase of over 200 per cent.

REFERENCE AND INFORMATION WORK

In the area of reference and information work also, the absence of data other than for individual libraries makes generalization difficult. A breakdown of over a quarter-million questions asked during 1958–59 in the Indianapolis Public Library showed that 195,000 of 260,000 questions were asked in person, 25 per cent by children. Of the 65,000 questions received by telephone, 10 per cent came from children.[24] A review of 153 reference and information questions received in the Main Library Children's Department at Racine shows the following distribution: (1) elementary and junior high school students, 62 per cent; (2) adults, including teachers and parents, 34 per cent; and (3) high-school students, 4 per cent.[25]

It seems beyond question that school-related reference service is definitely on the increase. Reference and information

[22] Ibid., pp. 8–9.

[23] Unpublished data gathered by F. L. Mills.

[24] Public Library Abstracts, Vol. 1, No. 2 (April, 1960), No. 60–107.

[25] Unpublished data gathered by F. L. Mills.

inquiries in the Main Children's Room of the Racine Public Library have nearly tripled from 1950 to 1961. Among the generalizations that can be made are these: (1) There has been a marked increase in homework assignments, even in the middle grades. (2) Reference questions asked in the Children's Room have become much more detailed and specific. (3) Reference assistance to children, formerly begun in Grades V and VI, now is being given to third-graders. (4) The development of an accelerated program in school systems involves "research" assignments among pupils in Grades V–VIII.

The Los Angeles Public Library survey, "Student Use of the Library," referred to earlier, provides a great deal of useful informaton to those interested in the student use of public libraries for reference and study purposes. The data concerning the community branches comparable in size and available materials to the medium-sized public library seem relevant here. Over three-fourths of the students from junior high school through college using the branches reported that they had not used the school library. Among the reasons suggested by the editors of the survey are several that are quite familiar to many of us, among them school bus schedules, extra-curricular activities, part-time jobs, convenience of public library location, and attractiveness of the library, especially in the evening.[26]

Analysis of the survey data revealed that nearly three-fourths of the questions presented by students were answered satisfactorily. Questions not answered fell into four categories: (1) the material required was already in use, (2) a search of reasonable length of time failed to locate the information, (3)

there was no material in the collection, available answers were too simple, or the question was obscure, and (4) only reference material was available, when circulating books were required. Further reference to this study will be made later.

Before leaving the consideration of reference service, I should note the striking increase in what might be called utilitarian reading. This was demonstrated in the Newark, New Jersey, survey, previously cited. This trend toward utilitarian reading with its emphasis on facts and information is evident in reference service to children as well as to young people and adults. Eric Moon, in a recent *Library Journal* editorial, noted this growing emphasis upon "information, source material, reference." He wrote: "One of the terrible dangers in our society, and in its educational processes, is that the fact too often seems to be elevated above the idea. People are being trained to look for answers rather than being taught how to ask questions."[27]

As serious as the long-run implication of the failure to ask the right question may be for the proper growth and development of the individual, the short-run prospect from another point of view is even more unsettling. In *Cybernation: The Silent Conquest*, a recent report to the Center for the Study of Democratic Institutions, Donald N. Michael points out how the use of the computer in dealing with social problems or questions may seriously *limit* the nature or field of the inquiry. He comments that computers are

so useful for dealing with social situations that pertain to people in the mass that they undoubtedly will help to seduce planners into

[26] "Student Use of the Library," p. 5.

[27] *Library Journal,* LXXXVIII (July, 1962). 2500.

inventing a society with goals that can be dealt with in the mass rather than in terms of the individual. In fact, the whole trend toward cybernation can be seen as an effort to remove the variabilities in man's on-the-job behavior and off-the-job needs which, because of their non-statistical nature, complicate production and consumption. Thus, somewhere along the line, the idea of the individual may be completely swallowed up in statistics.[28]

GROUP PROGRAMS

With respect to group programs, there appears to be little evidence that radically new or different kinds of programs for children are being introduced. The traditional story hour (now not infrequently supplemented by foreign-language story hours for children in the middle grades), the summer reading program, film programs—these still appear to be the principal programs in the medium-sized library. There seems to be some development in book discussion programs for the junior high school student, held in the library or prepared for radio broadcast.

One searches recent library literature in vain for accounts of programs for young adults sponsored by the medium-sized public library. Large libraries frequently develop programs for high-school students, such as the "Roads to World Understanding" at the Cleveland Public Library. As of 1956, this program, planned around panel discussions and featured entertainment, was in its eleventh successful season.[29]

Some effort has been made to develop programs for out-of-school young people. Several years ago the Racine Public Library attempted unsuccessfully to organize an American Heritage discussion group for such persons. The planning and execution of such programs are, by public library standards, quite expensive. The Detroit Public Library demonstrated this in its ambitious program of several years ago, "Backgrounds for Successful Living for Independent Young People."[30] A $10,000 subgrant from the Fund for Adult Education underwrote the project and made possible a full-time project director with a clerical assistant. In addition, the library provided 300 hours of professional help, 220 hours of clerical help, and 30 hours of page help. Letters were written to 2,200 of the 5,000 young people who dropped out of Detroit public high schools the year before graduation, and contacts were made with personnel and employment people in Detroit industry with a view to attracting young people aged sixteen to twenty-one with or without a high-school diploma. At the first of five specially planned programs, only fifty young people were registered, and during the remaining four programs, one hundred more attended. At the close of the series, forty-eight registrants received certificates for attendance at three or more of the programs. The cost, exclusive of time donated by the library, was over $66 per registrant and over $200 per certificate winner.

Each public library of whatever size must decide for itself whether to engage in programming for young people, just as it must decide whether or not to offer programs for adult readers. If it undertakes programs for young adults, the medium-sized library must decide whether to use its limited resources in working with the student enrolled in high school or to make an effort to reach

[28] *Cybernation: The Silent Conquest* (Report to the Center for Democratic Institutions [Santa Barbara, Calif., 1962]), p. 37.

[29] *Library Journal,* LXXXI (May 15, 1956), 1290–91.

[30] *Report of Detroit Public Library Youth Project for Out-of-School Young People* (Detroit: Detroit Public Library, 1955).

the dropout or recent graduate as well. One cannot escape the strong suspicion that just as our adult programs so often reach those who already read and who already are either active in or related to numerous community organizations, so the public library youth program frequently enlists the energies of the student who already has numerous organizational commitments and ties, both in and out of school, including junior symphonies, language clubs, the high-school service clubs, the YMCA, YWCA, the CYO, and church supper clubs.

After agreeing that our first duty is to those who read, who use library facilities, who appreciate the exchange of ideas and opinions based on reading or viewing, the question returns: Does the public library have an obligation to young people to whom these activities are not especially meaningful and who, moreover, may not be significantly related to the organized life of the community?

SCHOOL LIBRARIES

I stated earlier that library service to children and young people must include, what would have seemed twenty years ago, a disproportionate share of attention to educational matters. I have tried to show, by implication at least, some effect of the increased enrolments and the changed curriculums and methods of teaching on public library use. Another cause of the increased use of the public library is the wide gap that separates the need for library materials and services generated by the curriculum and teaching methods and the capacity of the school library to meet those needs.

More than thirty years ago, Helen Fargo's *The School Library* was published. How delighted and comforted public librarians were at the suggestion that the library was, or might become, the heart of the school. Those were words that we both loved and understood, even though it seems doubtful that the school library was then the heart of the school.

Disregarding the past, consider this brief sketch of the library of a large high school located in one of the nation's wealthiest states. The school enrolment was twenty-five hundred students. The seating capacity of the library was 150, 6 per cent of the enrolment. The size of the book collection was not given, but if the perimeter of the room were completely equipped with seven-foot wall shelving, making no allowance for doors or windows, the library could accommodate approximately 14,000 volumes, about six per student. The staffing consisted of one full-time librarian who had six hours weekly of teacher help; two additional hours weekly of teacher time were assigned to accommodate and supervise audio-visual equipment; fifty student assistants worked for class credit. The library does have the advantage of central processing and ordering services.[31]

The National Education Association research study, *The Secondary-School Teacher and Library Services,* published in 1958, reports considerable data concerning the staffing, services, and other aspects of the high-school library.[32] Below are summarized some of the findings of this study that, we may be sure, have a bearing on the increased use of the public library by high-school students.

[31] Irving E. Lane, "An Administrator Looks at the Library," *Bulletin of the National Association of Secondary-School Principals,* XLIII (November, 1959), 58 ff.

[32] Washington, D.C.: Research Division, National Education Association, 1958.

Of 219 secondary schools enrolling 1,500–1,999 students, less than half (45.2 per cent) had one full-time librarian; one-third had two full-time librarians; only 4 per cent had three or more full-time librarians. To quote from the survey: "One of the surprising things found in the study is the high percentage of teachers in large schools that employed only a single full-time librarian."

Fifteen per cent of the libraries in schools enrolling 1,500–1,999 are closed before classes begin; 11 per cent are closed after school and nearly 50 per cent are closed during the lunch hour. In 19 per cent of these schools the students may *not* use the library at any time even with approval of the classroom teacher.

Over one-third (37.5 per cent) of the teachers responding reported that materials in their major teaching areas obtainable in their school libraries were fair to poor. The most adequately supplied libraries were those in schools enrolling 1,500–1,999 students.

Information about school library periodical holdings is pertinent to this discussion. Miss Sara Fenwick in her revealing study of high-school and public library facilities in Chicago suburban areas notes two or three instances in which school library periodical holdings are limited to runs of three to five years.[33] If such limited runs are typical, the limitation explains the considerable student use of public library periodical collections. James E. Bryan, Newark librarian, analyzed 548 periodical requests believed to come from high-school students and reported that one-third of them were for seventy-three

separate titles dated from the nineteenth century through 1949; by far the largest share, of course, fell in the span 1900–1949.[34]

A good case can be made for the education of teachers to include practice in the technique of locating information as well as a comprehensive knowledge of printed materials appropriate to their subjects. For nearly 75 per cent of the teachers, instruction in the role and function of the library in the secondary-school program was either omitted entirely or treated only incidentally in their preparatory courses. In support of the proposition that every high-school pupil, not only the college-bound, should be given training in the use of the library, a high-school principal wrote:

If we search our memories honestly, some of us may recall our own timid reluctance to enter the vaulted silence of a public or college library. Why? Because we didn't really *know* *how* to find the material we needed. The basic library tools such as the card catalog and the *Reader's Guide* were unexplored mysteries. The arrangement of books on the open shelves was another puzzle.[35]

This lack of training perhaps helps to explain certain other findings of the National Education Association's research study. Of the teachers responding, 61.9 per cent indicated that they seldom or never planned with the school librarian "class visits to the library to stimulate pupils to develop skills and reading tastes." Over one-fourth of the teachers rarely gave a class assignment that required student use of library materials. Does this help to explain the number of

[33] "School and Public Library Relationships," *Library Quarterly*, XXX, No. 1 (January, 1960), 66, 68.

[34] "The Christmas Holiday Jam . . . ," *op. cit.*, p. 528.

[35] John B. Wilkins, "Library Instruction ←→ Curriculum Must," *Bulletin of the National Association of Secondary-School Principals*, XLIII (November, 1959), 130.

students ill-equipped for independent work that requires bibliographic tools and library resources?

One-third of the teachers reported that they seldom or never consulted with the librarian when planning new units of work. If the school librarian is so frequently unaware of teacher planning, it is not surprising that the student will be unsuccessful in finding the appropriate materials in his school library.

The library itself was frequently handicapped by not having information beforehand that might have enabled it to supply materials to elementary-school pupils on such subjects as the Yang-Na Indians, the history of the serape, or the cross-bow.[36] Not infrequently, the lack of available information resulted from the assignment of a too-specialized topic, as, for example, at the junior high school level, "Voting since 600 B.C.," "French Court Life in the Seventeenth Century," or "Diseases in Africa."[37]

Other assignments required unusual or difficult source materials. The Los Angeles survey reported an assignment that required the compilation of a list of words to be defined, using a source other than the dictionary; another ruled out the use of the encyclopedia even when the information sought was most readily located there.[38]

The citations from the Los Angeles survey should be interpreted not as criticism of the school library but rather as indications of how much remains to be done. Considerable progress has already been made. During 1941–58 book expenditures per pupil doubled—from

$0.46 (really $0.81, to account for the reduced purchasing power of the dollar) to $1.60. The number of volumes per student in high-school libraries increased from five to six.[39] School librarians have also been better trained; whereas only 42 per cent had as much as fifteen hours of library training in 1941, the comparable percentage for 1958 was 66.[40] The ratio of librarian to students dropped from 1:1,165 to 1:888 (still some distance from the new school library standard of 1:300).[41]

All things considered, we must conclude that the school library is still poorly prepared in materials, staff, and general facilities to meet the requirements imposed by larger enrolments and changes in curriculum and teaching methods. Bryan's comments in his inaugural address as president of the American Library Association suggest that the public library, too, is not well prepared to meet the pupil demands of today and tomorrow. Nevertheless, we may take comfort in the following developments:

1. Election to the presidency of ALA of a librarian keenly aware of the problem and determined to bring it to the attention of the entire profession;

[36] "Student Use of the Library," p. 7.

[37] *Ibid.,* p. 8.

[38] *Ibid.,* p. 9.

[39] United States Department of Health, Education, and Welfare, Office of Education, *Biennial Survey of Education in the United States, 1938–40 and 1940–42,* Vol. II: *Statistics of Public-School Libraries, 1941–42* (Washington, D.C.: Government Printing Office, 1945), chap. viii, p. 29; and United States Department of Health, Education, and Welfare, Office of Education, Library Services Branch, *Public School Library Statistics, 1958–59* (OE-15020 [Washington, D.C.: Government Printing Office, October, 1960]), p. 2.

[40] United States Department of Health, Education, and Welfare, Office of Education, *Statistics of Public-School Libraries, 1941–42,* p. 22, Table 17, and United States Department of Health, Education, and Welfare, Office of Education, *Public School Library Statistics, 1958–59,* p. 3.

[41] *Ibid.*

2. Publication in 1960 of *Standards for School Library Programs,* the work of a group broadly representative of the interests of both elementary and secondary education;

3. The publication in 1961 of "Responsibilities of State Departments of Education for School Library Services: A Policy Statement," by the Council of Chief State School Officers.

Perhaps too much emphasis has been placed in the past on co-operation per se in our discussions of school and public library relationships. It has sometimes been assumed that the gap between status and need could be bridged by a willing spirit and improved communication. Certainly these can do much to reduce the gap, but the best will in the world cannot in itself enlarge a reading room, provide more books, add a trained staff. Only money can accomplish these things. However sanguine our hopes, they will not be fulfilled until we realize President Bryan's recommendation that a greater share of the national product be devoted to the tools of learning, and make possible "a framework of libraries that will make these tools available to the greatest number who need and will use them."[42]

[42] *Publishers' Weekly,* July 9, 1962, p. 28.

PUBLIC LIBRARY SERVICE TO ADULTS

JEROME CUSHMAN

LIBRARIANS have devoted a great deal of attention to the role of their institution; citizens by and large, on the other hand, have apparently worried much less about it. A dozen years ago the Public Library Inquiry found that the library evoked a favorable image; the library was seen as a positive good—this in spite of the fact that librarians have always had to fight for sufficient support. The hard, cold reality remains that the library is a rather small incident in community life. As Dan Lacy wrote: "To a greater extent than any of us likes to admit, it is still true that most of the library's efforts in most communities goes to serve the somewhat marginal needs of a rather small minority of citizens."[1]

Nevertheless we do have substantial evidence to testify to steady progress in library support and use. Operating expenditures increased from $109,777,000 in 1950 to $170,223,000 in 1956. In the same years the population served rose from 114,965,730 to 117,607,364. Other evidence of growth and expansion is plentiful,[2] and no one can question the increasing activity in providing services and books and other materials. It is no longer unusual for a medium-sized library to provide a film program, to issue framed prints, to circulate phonograph records. Comprehensive service to the business community is no longer

the prerogative solely of the large library in a metropolitan area. Whatever their limitations, figures of circulation are impressive; in 1956 our public libraries ran up a reported total of 489,-519,000. (Lest this figure makes for complacency, we should note that in per capita terms it amounts to 4.16, in contrast to the British figure of 8.5.)

Whatever value the library has to its community rests in the significance of its services. Only a few of these services can here be considered. We shall look at reading in general, at paperbacks, at adult education. And finally we shall raise the question whether or not the library may move in certain directions that might increase its significance to the people it serves. Joyce Cary wrote in *Except the Lord:*

> Men who for some reason of fear or vanity take care to ask no questions that cannot be answered with a slide rule . . . take padded seats in the stalls and raise critical eyebrows at the circus which is the agony of the world.

The public library, for all its sheltered climate, is part of the agony of the world and should be examined in that light.

ENCOURAGEMENT OF SIGNIFICANT READING

The cultivation of a legitimate reading habit suffuses the entire fabric of librarianship, yet very little is known about how this is achieved. All of us are of course interested in "meaningful reading," but we know that what is highly meaningful to one may be a complete blank to another. I recall a young

[1] "Public Relations Specifics for the 1960's," *ALA Bulletin,* LV (June, 1961), 559.

[2] Cf. "Library Statistics," *The Bowker Annual of Library and Book Trade Information* (New York: R. R. Bowker Co., 1962), pp. 3–36.

lieutenant's personal prescription to the effect that a reading of the poetry of Robert W. Service told him all he needed to know about women. Whatever he needed to know, certainly to him Robert Service was highly meaningful. We know that library reading encompasses a spectrum that may include dabbling in mathematical puzzles, Proust, or *Lolita*. Reading may be pursued to satisfy a curiosity, check up on a bet, or increase one's knowledge. We have a firm faith that many of our patrons use reading for creative leisure, without quite knowing what we ourselves mean by that term. Still, a great deal more attention might well be paid to the encouragement of reading for its own sake.

Almost half our total library circulation consists of children's books, yet vast numbers of our children, on reaching adulthood, shun the institution. The Michigan "Reading for Life" conference of 1958 emphasized the college teacher's influence in building lifetime reading habits, and it would seem that librarians, too, have a great opportunity to stimulate readers by judicious advice and encouragement. It is in the area of recommending books to receptive adults that I believe the public library of the future will make its strongest impact. Individual attention by skilled staff, taking an adult on a real lifetime adventure of the mind and spirit, is the kind of action that justifies the library's existence.

But the problem of finance and book budgets immediately presents itself, particularly for medium-sized libraries. Most of them would hesitate to purchase certain kinds of books because of the small number of readers they would attract. And yet the librarians *must* make certain key decisions in which

book quality is not ignored because of a limited audience. When I was librarian of Salina, Kansas, a city of 45,000 with a book budget of $17,000, we decided to purchase fewer "recreational" books—books for casual enjoyment—in favor of more liberal purchases of more substantial, though less popular, volumes. Of course we might have purchased more generously in business, perhaps subscribing to the costly stock market services, but the librarian was convinced that a prime though not exclusive obligation of his institution was to provide reading matter of superior quality. This conviction may have resulted from the experience of having patrons tell him of their surprise and delight at finding books which they never expected to find. (Parenthetically, we may note that many such books are not found in even larger libraries.) Undoubtedly such reactions helped persuade the librarian that the range of reading matter provided by his library should be broader than was conventionally expected.

The first step in encouraging the reading of superior books is to make them available. To us it seemed important to bring the opportunity for such reading to our community. The library made it a point to purchase the entire UNESCO art series, even though the cost of $22.50 per volume put a real strain on the budget. The acquisition of volumes containing decorations on Coptic churches, wall paintings of the Australian aborigines, the art of medieval Norway, esoteric as they may seem, could be justified on the score of their potential ability to broaden horizons. Also, in spite of its cost ($50.00), the three-volume set of the letters of Vincent Van Gogh was considered a "must." These letters might lead the reader to the drawings and paintings of Van Gogh in the Phaidon and other editions, perhaps thence to a New York Graphic print of the bridge at Arles, or to records of Belgian contemporary music which had been sent us by the Belgian government, and conceivably to the glories of Flemish art and similar high spots all along the ladder of civilization. We do not know how many persons took such a trip, but we suspect that several did—all because of the initial stimulation provided by some letters written out of the tortured soul of Vincent Van Gogh.

We hear a great deal about the current revival of interest in religion, and the publishing houses reflect this interest in their lists. While the library should be wary of purchasing books of the "how-to-get-felicity-with-the-help-of-five-clichés" type, much can be said in favor of book acquisition in the religious field, an area in which libraries tend to play it safe. Such writers as Reinhold Niebuhr, Emil Brunner, Martin Buber, Jacques Maritain, and Karl Barth are in the forefront of the intellectual and theological ferment of our times, and our library purchased widely from their works. At the same time we obtained an extensive collection of Søren Kierkegaard, the intellectual godfather of many of today's theologians. Are books in religious philosophy too specialized for a medium-sized library? On the contrary, such books are essential.

Contemporary poetry, like contemporary science, presents a baffling array of choices. Should the medium-sized library stick to the anthologies, plus a few standards like Frost and Cummings? Should not the library have the Pulitzer Prize volumes in poetry, even before the prizes are announced? What about the young poets on the way to recognition? Do we purchase the Yale Younger Poets Series? Do we purchase enough to encourage Alan Swallow of Denver to continue publishing the hitherto unknown poets? What about the so-called "beatniks"? Do we write off Ferlinghetti, Duncan, Corso? Such poets should not go unnoticed by the medium-sized library. They speak with new rhythms, new accents, new motivations. They believe America is lethargic and they want to jolt us out of our complacency. They may shock us, just as Beethoven may have shocked auditors who expected him to sound like Haydn.

Though poetry does not loom large in the circulation statistics, it commands an audience; the barbaric yawp of Whitman, the metaphoric passion of Dylan Thomas, the songlike beauty of Cummings—all continue to attract readers. Perhaps some of the younger poets will not last—but neither will most of the fiction on our shelves. The important thing is that we give our public an opportunity to get acquainted with them.

Our library followed with interest the paperback publishing experiment of Macmillan and Wesleyan University, and we regret, with others, that Indiana University, according to a recent report, plans to discontinue its excellent poetry series. Nor should we overlook the specialized publishers, many of whom have issued extremely interesting works. New Directions has published a great deal of Kenneth Patchen, and the fabulous City Lights Bookshop of San Francisco has issued numerous works of the most manly and human of poets. We believed that the provision of such poetry was a way of keeping in step with our literary tradition; we believe it is appropriate for any medium-sized public library.

Do libraries devote enough attention to encouraging the reading of fiction? Generally we depend upon best-seller lists, our own bibliographies, and the natural drawing power of fiction. For some reason we still experience great satisfaction when our reports indicate that non-fiction outpulls fiction in circulation. This attitude toward fiction seems altogether too snobbish. Though we sometimes bask in the reflected glory of a newly arrived novelist, we would probably find that our libraries contain none of his earlier books, simply because they were not included on recommended purchase lists. A too-slavish adherence to book reviews often prevents a librarian from experiencing the pleasure that comes from the discovery of a bright and unusual talent. True, an author's early work frequently suffers from lack of coherence, overenthusiasm, preoccupation with autobiography, and—sin of sins—overwriting; but the librarian should ask if clarity of vision, honesty of feeling, vigor of the language, and signs of literary promise override its obvious faults. Though reviewers are often charitable, librarians sometimes become too preoccupied with the negative elements which may be noted in the review, and the public may thus lose the opportunity to become acquainted with a fresh talent.

Let me here insert a word about the relation between the physical book and the act of reading. Many years ago a relative bought us, to our ecstatic delight, a complete set of Dickens. The books were printed in double columns, the binding was artificial grassgreen, the letters flaky-gold, the paper autumn-brown. Though ecstatic, we did not read a single volume. Some years later a Heritage Press edition of *David Copperfield* came to my attention and I read it. (Please do not chide me for the delay; I still have not read *Tale of Two Cities!*)

Librarians are generally well intentioned; they *mean* to discard the fine-print classics which have come by gift, but low budgets inhibit wholesale discarding of standard titles and their replacement with well-printed and attractive editions. Yet such physically attractive books promote interest and encouragement which may spell the difference between a book read and unread.

THE REFERENCE FUNCTION OF THE MEDIUM-SIZED LIBRARY

I doubt if there is anything unique about the reference function and services of the medium-sized library. Most of the questions it receives may be answered out of a relatively small number of reference tools, and intimate knowledge of the scope and arrangement of such tools is more important than a vastly larger collection which may be assembled if a generous budget is provided. Having said this much, I might add that in my opinion the reference function of the medium-sized library is due for re-evaluation. How far can the library go in its reference service to school children? It is not so much a question of whether or not the library is able to provide such service as it is one of determining whether service to one group results in the neglect of others. One might ask, for example, to what extent the library serves as a resource for the government officials of its community. Except for occasional calls from City Hall, this is a largely unserved group; and now that most medium-sized cities are grappling with problems of streets, sewage, population growth, business expansion, schools, housing, and the like, the library is in a position to assist in their solution. Other population groups are also in need of intensive reference assistance, and they are in danger of being neglected if too much attention is devoted to school children.

Even before such re-evaluation takes place, the library can strengthen its reference resources in at least two areas. One is government documents. Libraries which are not depositories frequently fail to realize the infinite riches such documents contain; and because of the interest of the government in so many aspects of scientific development, the documents often contain the latest and most accurate information. Many libraries check the biweekly *Selected U.S. Government Publications,* and consult the *Monthly Catalog* only for the occasional, somewhat specialized, inquiry. While documents initially cost little or nothing, their acquisition and preparation are time-consuming and expensive; furthermore, documents experts are scarce. Nevertheless we would do well to rethink our government documents acquisition program with a view to strengthening our collections.

Since the medium-sized library cannot possibly keep up to date in all subjects, it would do well to depend on bibliographies. Through such tools useful books may readily be identified and frequently obtained on interlibrary loan. In many sections of the country the proximity of specialized reference libraries—for example, the Linda Hall Library in Kansas City, the Crerar in Chicago—may relieve the public library of the necessity of going very deeply into the provision of expensive and little-used reference materials, and through the use of bibliographies the library may be in a position to advise the patron about many books which he may and probably can find not far away.

At this point I should like to comment on the act of reading. This is a noisy country, and in many homes it is difficult to provide the atmosphere of quiet that reading requires. The jangling of radio, record-player, and television is ever present. Unfortunately, many public libraries have caught the infection of twentieth-century cacophony. A kind of department-store promotion has been adopted to attract the public and to induce them to sample our intellectual fare. A Swedish colleague has observed that the mind deserves the cloistered restfulness of silence to permit concentration without external distractions; we agree. This is not a call to the return of the finger-on-the-lips days, but merely recognition that silence is rare and it should be nurtured. Somehow or other, a line from "The Listeners" comes to mind: "How the silence surged softly backward. . . ."

Can we identify distinctive reading trends in medium-sized libraries? Probably not. Circulation records are likely to reflect patterns of community interest which do not vary too sharply from one city to another. Even the identification of the quality of reading in medium-sized libraries is difficult. What is read depends on the tastes of readers and on what the librarian makes available to them. The reader may be fortunate enough to live in a community with a deep cultural commitment, a commitment likely to be reflected in his library's collections. But in any community the librarian with a broad cultural interest may stimulate a similar interest through his book purchases. Make no mistake about it—the orientation of a library is discernible to the most casual patron. The library is a true reflection of the librarian—his tastes, interests, and his zeal for promoting reading of a superior type.

THE IMPACT OF THE PAPERBACK BOOK

Now I wish to comment on the impact of the paperback on our libraries. For the first time paperbacks offer a ray of hope for the library to supply, completely and speedily, community demand for books of high quality. The University of Washington is conducting an experiment with saturation buying of paperbacks to take care of student needs, an experiment that should be watched by public librarians with great interest. In our efforts to increase the number of readers we have frequently been frustrated by inadequate finances; numerous requests for the same book at the same time have had to be denied or postponed because of our single-copy purchase policy. Perhaps the paperback will help to break down this limitation and permit a much greater degree of purchasing in multiple copies.

Though paperbacks hold out promise to the solution of the problem of multiple-copy needs, there seems to be little evidence that libraries are doing much about them. Many librarians take the position that paperbacks are useful to strew about in various browsing corners in order to attract the attention of the curious. On the contrary, the paperback should be taken at its true worth—as a book that may appropriately fit into the collection, properly bound, classified, and cataloged.

Some libraries are already doing this. For example, the issuance of the paperbound *Rise and Fall of the Third Reich* relieved many librarians, who hurriedly ordered ten copies or more to cut down the size of the reservation lists. There is some hope that simultaneous publishing of hardbound and paper-bound titles is in the offing. All this will contribute to making book collections more viable and more serviceable to that portion of the public which demands "something new to read." To them, at least, this is still the most important function of the public library.

It is in adult education that the paperback may really come into its own. To cite only one illustration, a library in a community of less than 50,000 prepared a list of one hundred paperbacks. With this list as a point of departure, members of the community were invited to form groups of eight to ten, to meet monthly for the purpose of discussing one of the listed titles at each meeting. Choice of titles was left to them, as well as the responsibility of obtaining the books. In less than a month eleven groups were organized, and they talked about such books as *The Catcher in the Rye, A Taste of Honey,* and *Teacher in America.* Any library might sponsor such a program, and the availability of the paperbacks makes it altogether feasible.

We have already commented on the demands school children make on the reference service of the public library. From October to May service to adults is handicapped because of the necessity of serving the school population. It is at least possible that paperbacks will enable school libraries to build up their resources, thus relieving to some extent the pressures on public libraries. Clearly, co-operation between libraries and schools cannot be long delayed; the sooner both tackle the issue of library service to children and students, the better the possibilities of satisfying all community interests and of performing appropriate library functions.

ADULT EDUCATION IN THE MEDIUM-SIZED LIBRARY

Today, probably more so than a decade ago, adult education is accepted as a proper library function, however little libraries do about it. The librarian is subject to formidable pressures of many kinds, not the least of which is the steady demand for information on all sorts of subjects. This, coupled with the demands of the school population and staff shortages everywhere, results in reduced attention to adult education as such. If the number of entries under "Adult Education" in *Library Literature* may be taken as an index of interest, we may contrast the seventy-seven entries in the 1955–57 volume with only twenty-two in 1958–60. Apparently the enthusiasm about adult education seems to have abated.

To some this may suggest that the medium-sized library should renounce altogether the responsibility for adult education, particularly in the light of financial limitations and critical staff problems. Others, however, would decry the discontinuance of a concern with adult education. Perhaps the solution may lie somewhere between these extremes. The library caught between limited staff and funds and ever-increasing demands for books and information services might well re-examine its role in adult education. Some programs designed merely to bring people into the library building have doubtful value, unless they actually result in reading. "Co-operating" with the extension department of the local university in presenting, say, ten weeks of law for the real estate agent frequently adds up to no more, from the library standpoint, than making the premises available for "adult education." For my part, I believe that library administrators should think of adult education as specifically book-centered, and adult education programs should emphasize intellectual stimulation rather than practical applications. An evening of poetry reading in which a postal clerk, a history professor, and a musician participate comes closer to the library's basic purpose than a course in the art of rapid reading.

Incidentally, let us not minimize the effectiveness of library staff members as potential leaders in adult education, even though they may lack the expert knowledge of the specialist. All too often the specialist, precisely because of his expertness, fails to communicate with his audience. What a staff member may lack in sophistication in certain fields he may compensate for by enthusiasm, warmth, sympathy, and clarity. I believe, too, that perhaps too much is made of efforts at co-ordination in adult-education programming. An administrator, faced with the prospect of numerous time-consuming meetings, may choose to brush aside the idea of co-ordination altogether rather than endure the trials of getting a committee to agree on an acceptable program. Many successful programs have been arranged on the basis of a few telephone calls. A very simple program may readily be arranged in the following way:

1. Decide to devote an evening to American poetry.

2. Do not allow yourself to be swayed by the size of the potential audience, whether it be five or fifty.

3. Select no more than three or four potential leaders, and permit them to choose the poet, or poets, they wish to read.

4. Set the date.

5. Use either a simple announcement or a limited mailing to persons likely to be interested.

6. See that the room is set up properly.

It is of course possible to establish evaluative criteria that very few adult-education programs could meet. How evaluate the library's function in this area: by size of participation, by persistence of the program, by publicity received, by letters of appreciation? The program should be evaluated as the library itself is evaluated. Has it contributed its mite to civilization? Has it lifted a single human heart? Has it provided illumination to even a few people? Such considerations transcend evidence based on numbers.

Next, a word about the library's reach into its community. We have always accepted the responsibility of serving the business community, labor, hospitals, women's clubs, senior citizens, religious groups, and the host of other elements that make up our towns and cities. Clearly, the greater the number of such groups that may be involved in a library relationship, the better for both community and library. Our functions are broad, and we are happy when we contribute to the fisherman's competence in fly-tying or to the department-store manager's mastery of the fundamentals of public speaking. Such contributions as we make are all part of the image we project. Many years ago, long before television, one medium-sized library provided a weekly program of recorded music. Notes were prepared, coffee served, and a dedicated group of ten or fifteen attended regularly. One day the librarian was stopped on the street by a member of the city council who remarked on the importance of the program to the cultural life of the city, even though he himself had never attended a single concert. He was familiar with the image, and to him it was extremely favorable.

Though the library must appeal to broad community interests, serious thought must be given to the extent of programming. All too often the medium-sized library tries to do too much, attempting to emulate the services given by a large institution staffed with specialists. The result may be multiple-duty assignments at the expense of basic library functions. The library should not attempt to do more than its resources and facilities permit. Better to keep the community as a whole in focus than to emphasize service to isolated groups.

THE ROLE OF THE MEDIUM-SIZED LIBRARY

What is the mission of the medium-sized library? Our responsibilities have tended increasingly toward specialization—perhaps a reflection of our national preoccupation with things rather than ideas. Yet it is in the realm of ideas that, in the long run, the library will make its most telling contribution. There is little need to repeat the library's basic tasks; its informational, educational, and cultural responsibilities have been discussed in almost every imaginable context. I believe, however, that the medium-sized library—and *all* libraries for that matter—should stress *ideas* rather than "things," "facts," "specifics." Let us gear our program to *individuals,* whether independent or group-associated. This can be done without surrendering the necessity of attention to "factual" information. Nor does it imply a shift from the practical to the ethereal. The library that is truly practical will embrace the function of a community information center *and* that of a center for the inculcation and spread of ideas.

Because of the explosive power of ideas incorporated in print, the library may be regarded as even a dangerous institution. People of all ages are seeking, questioning, and acting on the stimuli provided by books that free libraries provide. This is something that must be reckoned with by all who would set artificial limits to man's aspirations. We should welcome the opportunity of serving as the custodian and promulgator of ideas, for in the last analysis we thus help to sow the seeds that will enable our country to face a constantly changing tomorrow.

The public library will find its true vocation as a generalist rather than specialist. Its appeal must focus on the absolute necessity of the community's responding to the challenge of the future. The librarian must help to build a generation of idea- rather than fact-centered individuals; it has the opportunity to perform a vital role in the agony of the twentieth century, by helping to damp the fires of change from flaming destruction to soothing warmth.

BOOK SELECTION AND THE COMMUNITY LIBRARY

RAY SMITH

THE medium-sized public library represents the community dimension in library service. Potentially, it allows creative relations with books and readers alike, book selection both adequately responsive and sufficiently responsible. Indeed, the community library may become the wildlife refuge for imaginative literature when automated informatonal assembly lines swallow—as we are often told they will—the "Library of Tomorrow."

I wish to speak of book selection and the medium-sized library in terms of assumptions and issues as seen from my own vantage (and also no doubt disadvantage) point in such a library. First, this means for me consideration of imaginative reading and its present de-emphasis in favor of the informational; next, some prospects of the medium-sized library; and third, book selection and the community. Finally, I shall consider several issues of current and long-range concern.

The librarian like anyone else, but with greater effect, can register in himself and in his collection conformity and standardization of the mind; passivity before the living issues of his day and non-engagement "where that immortal garland is to be run for"; subservience to the machine values of efficiency and uniform response. Or he can steer by the polar star of human communion and the centrality for libraries of imaginative writing. He can declare a principal concern for that which engages the spirit, not the epidermis—affecting what Teilhard de Chardin has called "the hominisation of man."

READING AND THE IMAGINATION

Let us begin with the act of reading and the wide assumption that its purpose cannot but be informational, a function of the stopwatch-governed eye zooming down the highways of pages, indifferent to evocation and textural values. Reading speed must meet a certain minimum for literate comprehension—but comprehension of what? Do librarians ask this, or ask it enough, as they work at book selection or interpretation or reading programs? Often in our society the notion of any reading value other than the informational does not even arise. And a contributory de-emphasis on the imaginative does present itself in the public libraries.

Let me cite a typical instance of the widespread fad in speed-reading, glorifying the machine values of efficiency and uniform response at the expense of imaginative texture and connotative values. I quote from a newspaper article, "2,000 Words a Minute—Slow Reading at Keokuk":

Using a technique known as dynamic reading, there are seventh graders here who reportedly can read the novel *Barabbas* at 10,000 [*sic*] words per minute, then score 80 per cent in a comprehension test. . . .

Simply put, the new reading method, according to Hansen, means that the eyes travel about in the middle of the page and seek patterns of meaning on a page, rather than individual words. . . .

Hansen admits that the terrific speeds attained on novels would not be possible on, say, a science text. . . .

According to Hansen, some of his seventh grade pupils now check out 15 books a week from the public library.[1]

[1] *Des Moines Register*, May 7, 1962, p. 1.

Wherever exposed sensitivity remains, the unspoken assumptions here must pound at it: that information constitutes the meaning of the reading experience, in whatever form that reading comes; that fiction is inferior to nonfiction; that quantity ("15 books a week from the public library") constitutes a supreme value; and that the reader's destination can only be the last page. For true reading, joy is in the journey, in the reading process itself.

Randall Jarrell says, in *A Sad Heart at the Supermarket:* "Poetry disappeared long ago, even for most intellectuals; each year fiction is a little less important. Our age is an age of nonfiction; of gossip columns, interviews, photographic essays, documentaries."

As a notable example of library book selection, and for giving countenance to Mr. Jarrell's fears, the ALA Notable Books selections deserve attention. Notable books of 1959 included among forty-nine choices none in poetry and seven in fiction. Notable books of last year, 1961, included among fifty selections no poetry and seven books of fiction. In the intervening year, 1960, one book of poems appeared among forty-six titles—*Times Three* by Phyllis McGinley, accurately described as "A delightful collection of deft, light verse on an infinite variety of subjects." Eight works of fiction were on this selected list.

In the year of *Times Three,* collected verse, another *Collected Poems*—by Richard Eberhart—was published. Eberhart is a seer; McGinley, an able craftsman. *Vive la différence!*

ALA Notable Books has been, of course, a joint enterprise. For the 1961 selection, thirty-eight libraries participated, with final selection by twelve members of the ALA Council.

This bald recital confirms the fact that librarians are implicated in the pervasive de-emphasis of imaginative writing. And this de-emphasis must be read into public library book selection. Medium-sized and smaller libraries, I believe, choose a high proportion of their books within the orbit of library literature and library reviewing. Eric Moon, editor of *Library Journal,* observed in his study of " 'Problem' Fiction" that, although libraries polled for the article were not asked about review media, 41 of 113 replying "indicated that they relied solely or primarily upon published reviews" in selection. The top four sources named were *Library Journal* (21 times), *Kirkus* (13), *Booklist,* and *Saturday Review* (12 times each).[2] Though Moon's survey had range, most libraries included were large or of medium size. We may fairly conclude that smaller libraries, citing *Booklist* more frequently, would have revealed the same selection habits.

In part, then, the selection problem as it relates to reviewing must mean raising our sights with ourselves. It should also mean a larger admixture of individuality in choice and concern; a less resolute reliance, as one librarian who participated in selections for *Fiction Catalog* put it, on "what the stars portend" in *Standard Catalog for Public Libraries.*

The librarian, resisting currents of standardization and homogenizing response that, sweeping through the communication media, tend to hold the libraries in fee, can recall that imaginative books induce not conformity but questioning; lifting us from habitual modes, they reveal "the arbitrariness of

2 " 'Problem' Fiction," *Library Journal,* LXXXVII (February 1, 1962), 494.

the usual." They open other avenues of awareness and exploration.

André Malraux wrote in "The Cultural Heritage": "Every civilization is like the Renaissance, and creates its own heritage out of everything in the past that helps it to surpass itself. A heritage is not transmitted; it must be conquered; and moreover it is conquered slowly and unpredictably." The heritage of literature must be "conquered slowly"—not by speed readers; and books that make the heritage should be in libraries whether or not they receive wide current use.

The conformity cluster, like a Pandora's box of woes, releases a sequel thought. Does not the dictum "currently useful" sometimes reflect the notion of obsolescence built into some other products of our culture? As an extreme instance, one library program known to me sends out once-only rotating collections, dominated by a "new-titleism" not different in some ways from "best-sellerism." In this connection I remember another Jarrell observation from *A Sad Heart at the Supermarket*: "When one reads an abstract expressionist's remark that Washington studios are 'eighteen months behind' those of his colleagues in New York, one realizes something of the terrible power of business and fashion over those most overtly hostile to them."

Let us consider another aspect of the informational assembly line. In his recent book, *The Image, or What Happened to the American Dream*, Daniel J. Boorstin writes about American concern with what he calls pseudo (or synthetic) events and images, manufactured or triggered by their reporters to fill the insatiable needs of news and information outlets. In due course he observes of the best seller that it is "a book known primarily (sometimes exclusively) for its well-knownness." The book's epigraph comes from Max Frisch: "Technology . . . the knack of so arranging the world that we don't have to experience it." That would make an ideal banner for the informational assembly line, now identified with reading throughout the Keokuk systems of America.

The point of imaginative writing is that we *do* have to experience it. The stimulus to imagination is the greatest single value the public library can hold for its readers. The imaginative book, fiction or non-fiction, provides—as profound novels always have provided—a deep implicative awareness. This, not just another stop on the informational assembly line, not just another contribution to "the epidermal sense of life," makes the unique contribution of the public library among voices in the community and should dominate its book selection.

Indirection and textural richness appeal to the private percepton, the personal experience, not to units in a mass audience, and cannot be timed or graded for comprehension. Their implicit assertion is not speed up but slow down and read.

Behind the frequent library fetish of non-fiction as a good in itself, we may discern the kowtowing of the humanities today to social science; the assumption of its procedures as protective coloration in book creation and in book selection—and in librarianship.

One year ago, at the annual Graduate Library School conference, a professor of sociology held out this hope to librarians: "The increasing flow of knowledge and the greater dependence of a technological society on our accumulation of knowledge will augment the economic bargaining power of librarians. This in turn will heighten the caliber of recruits."[3] What the professor omitted from his entire tendentious paper was the very essence of community librarianship—the ministry of books. Perhaps he had only the largest libraries in mind. And perhaps what Justice William O. Douglas recently said about bigness applies to some big libraries:

> The growth of bigness has had crippling effects. A nation of independent businessmen has become a nation of clerks. . . . But corporations, like big government and big unions, breed non-controversial men and women. . . . There has been such a deadening effect of radio and TV on the American mind, that we may have reached a point where men and women who will sponsor unorthodox points of view must be subsidized by foundations.[4]

In the medium-sized library, at all events, the community librarian can, if he will, through book selection and book interpretation work as an active legislator in the free republic of books. What other equal dignity does his profession offer? He need not, I am confident, embrace information retrieval and its honorific automation-associated status as a passport to professional respect.

Let me close this catalog of the beleaguered imagination by noting that within the past year both the *Library Journal* and the *Wilson Library Bulletin* have, among other services rendered by their vigorous editors, given special attention to poetry in book selection: "Modern American Poetry, a Selected List for the Medium Size Library" by

Louis Untermeyer, and "The Poet as Patron," a symposium by Babette Deutsch and others.[5]

In order not to disturb the current of criticism that I have felt obliged to maintain, Untermeyer's list must be called very conventional, emphasizing poets like Van Doren, Winters, Wheelock, Hillyer, and himself. Rexroth made the second team but not Denise Levertov. With this inattention to the descendants (roughly) of Whitman and William Carlos Williams, Untermeyer will get to heaven with his list recommended for the medium-sized library, but without enough players on the other team for a good game. However, this attention must be counted an overdue service to book selection by a knowledgeable and careful worker in the vineyard.

THE PROSPECTS OF THE MEDIUM-SIZED LIBRARY

Now let me turn to an instance and some prospects of the medium-sized public library. The instance is that of my own Mason City, Iowa, public library and its new area extension trans-county program.

Iowa population centers show, as all the Midwest does, evidence of the hurried movement west, when settlement concentrated at river sites or trading points. As technology reduced rural employment, the smaller centers declined, or held on by widening their trade areas, or grew slowly by developing industry. Cities are generally small, and their libraries, to establish adequate service and financial support, expanded to embrace the trading areas and beyond. This is the present process.

---

[3] W. J. Goode, "The Librarian: From Occupation to Profession?" *Library Quarterly*, XXXI (October, 1961), 319.

[4] First Annual Lecture on Ethics and Human Relations at the University of Judaism as reported in "Finds Debate Curtailed by Conformity," *Des Moines Register,* July 2, 1962, p. 12.

[5] Respectively, in *Library Journal*, LXXXVII (June 1, 1962), 2084–5; and *Wilson Library Bulletin*, XXXVI (January, 1962), 365–71.

For between these prairie centers has existed the bypassed American cultural frontier. Frederick Jackson Turner's frontier was geographical—pointing to an area of unoccupied land and its recession westward—but this frontier is of the spirit. Its stages have been school consolidation, symbolized by the school bus and dwindling in numbers of the one-room school, and last of all the coming of the public library, stimulated by the Federal Library Services Act.

My own Mason City library, not far from midway across the northern Iowa counties, gives immediate service to a city and county rural population of about 45,000. Actual book expenditure last year approximated $16,000. Our semi-autonomous area program, with expenditures under Mason City administrative control, is officially called the Mason City Area Cooperative Library Program. Sparked by a field office of the Iowa State Traveling Library, it now reaches twenty-five small and very small libraries (serving centers below 10,000 population) with three-month rotating collections. Spending over $22,000 for books last year, it provides a selection, processing, and book distributing center, open to requests from participants and allowing for their areas of subject interest, supplies special reserves, and features unlimited interlibrary-loan access to the Mason City basic collection of 138,000 volumes. (The center's own collection now comprises 22,000 books, plus 5,000 on long-term loan from the state library.) Financed by federal, state, and participant-library funds, this program embraces an additional population area of over 50,000, bringing the total population reached by all book programs from the Mason City library to about 100,000.

Smaller libraries do not sacrifice autonomy by taking part in this area program; on the contrary, their range of reading provision has expanded to an extent inconceivable a few months ago. To participate, however, libraries must meet minimum standards of staff, operation, hours, and endeavor toward sustaining tax support (at the outset, especially, these standards are flexible). Initially they pay a per capita fee, town and rural, into the area program. Two examples of improvement, among many: In financial support, last year two counties within the area levied county-wide library taxes for the first time, and in services, two small libraries previously open six hours a week increased their hours to twenty a week, with new township tax support.

The state field representatives from the outset maintained a high standard for the area collection, with two results. First, there was a gradual increase in the provision of good books hitherto largely inaccessible to member libraries; second, good readers who had bypassed their local libraries and reading rooms have now begun to use them and to register their book interests with local librarians.

Library boards, sometimes reluctant to welcome federal and state concern, have come to realize (as did school authorities about consolidation) an irreversible involvement; that the issue is not whether, but how, this concern can best be used to serve the community.

Turning from this particular instance to general prospects of the medium-sized public library, we can look at the corroborative article, "Small and Medium-Sized Public Libraries," by Ransom L. Richardson.[6] Richardson de-

[6] In a special issue entitled "Future of Library Service: Demographic Aspects and Implications," *Library Trends*, X (October, 1961), 132–38.

fined the medium-sized public library as one serving 35,000 to 100,000 population. Libraries serving fewer than 35,000 usually cannot meet minimum standards for book collection, staff, and hours; and they must increasingly find themselves unable to do so. Richardson sees the solution in affiliations in order to create wider financial support. He argues that those responsible for the small public library should realize that centralizing some essential functions does not involve losing autonomy and ownership, whereas it can bring to the community enlarged and improved book service. The smallest library, becoming an outlet centered on direct reader assistance, can help in responsive book selection and at the same time obtain maximum effectiveness from its budget. As for the medium-sized library,

> The medium-sized community that serves as the center of a large area may well consider itself the nucleus in the establishment of a larger unit of service and may hope to strengthen its own service thereby. Where several medium-sized communities exist in relative proximity, some form of library consolidation or federation may be indicated. Again, the medium-sized library serving a suburban community may find cooperative or contractual arrangements with the central city productive of improved service.[7]

This is not the place to discuss future developments in our own area, but simply to indicate that trends there and elsewhere, with stimulus of the now expanding Federal Library Services Act, hold promise of such consolidation or federation (for us, perhaps, approximating the 100,000 population base of ALA standards), while maximizing autonomy and remaining within the medium-sized range.

The American trend to mammoth urbanization, with or without a cabinet post for urban affairs, will surely be countered increasingly by suburbanization for family living and the prospect of multiplying suburban community libraries. Of 8,190 public libraries in 1960, 7,282 served population areas under 35,000, 657 between 35,000 and 100,000. During the past ten years, growth in the number of centers in the medium-sized bracket, and potential growth in the next decades, may be adduced from the fact that places "in urban fringes with populations of 35,000 to 100,000 increased from 244 to 380," well over 50 per cent.[8]

The future growth and significance in the American library picture of medium-sized libraries seem assured; and they will be quickened by co-operative practices now in progress, drawing small libraries into the medium-sized service range. From the other direction, again, this prospect can be emphasized by growth of the suburban library related to the large urban library center. In both lies a larger possibility than librarianship has commonly known for more time for, and major concern with, book selection and its vital corollary, book interpretation.

BOOK SELECTION AND THE COMMUNITY

We pass on to our third topic, book selection and the community. Robert D. Leigh a dozen years ago presented a statistical correlation between budget and quality book selection. Whereas best sellers were purchased almost as readily by public libraries with total budgets below $10,000 as by those above that sum,

> The list of current fiction chosen by critics for quality presents a different story. In the groups with $25,000 budgets and more the average holdings were 67 to 69 per cent. But the average percentage held by the smaller

libraries was $10,000–$25,000, 42 per cent; $5,000–$10,000, 15 per cent; $2,500–$5,000, 11 per cent. On the critics' list was Cozzens' *Guard of Honor,* which received the Pulitzer Award as the year's best American novel some time after the libraries had checked the lists. All but one of the larger libraries (budgets over $25,000) had purchased the book; none of the libraries with budgets below $10,000 had done so.

The returns with regard to current nonfiction were similar in most respects to those for fiction.[9]

A recent ALA survey of growth and tastes in reading noted an increase in adult book circulation of 20 per cent in the past five years, with a shift in reading from westerns and mysteries toward cultural and scientific affairs; as might be guessed, it also found budget among the factors considered responsible (by "key libraries in towns of over 50,000"):

Increased book budgets, making more books on given topics available was a factor mentioned by 70% of the librarians; more traveling on the part of library patrons, also mentioned by 70%; the increased educational levels of readers by 60%. Many librarians mentioned population shifts and local increases in population as big reasons for rising use of the library. . . . Another important factor was increased use of public libraries in conjunction with school programs.[10]

For the smaller library, which was omitted from the ALA reading survey, we may assume that Leigh's conclusions remain correct. For the medium-sized community other determinants than budget may include direct supervision by the head librarian and his participation in book interpretation. Budget

size and quality of collection (much less accessibility) cannot be correlated absolutely.

In " 'Problem' Fiction," *Library Journal* editor Eric Moon comments:

A further analysis by size of library proved at least one thing—that the widest choice is not always to be found in the largest libraries. The only two libraries which offered the whole range of 20 titles were both smallish libraries serving less than 50,000 population—Bethpage, New York, and Fair Lawn, New Jersey. Two other small libraries that were well up, each with 16 of the 20 titles, were Salina, Kansas, and Mason City, Iowa.[11]

Since several titles of the caliber of *Return to Peyton Place* were included on the check list, the article concludes that good selection would not add up to 100 per cent of the "problem" titles.

Some studies have investigated the relation of library use to leaders of opinion in the community. Such indications should not be used, I believe, as exclusive selection criteria. Public library book selection should be both Jacksonian and Jeffersonian: it should take account both of the common taste and reading needs and of the "natural aristocracy" in taste and reading needs, with the latter a permanent directive influence. Though no medium-sized library can have everything, there should be ample provision of books on certain subjects, beyond responsive and responsible general coverage.

For books in which accuracy of information is required, such as medicine, co-operative inquiry by librarian and qualified professional people in the community may govern acquisition. Our library rejected a book on cancer, for instance, because of medical advice that it contained harmful misinformation. While never surrendering his preroga-

[9] R. D. Leigh, *The Public Library in the United States: The General Report of the Public Library Inquiry* (New York: Columbia University Press, 1950), p. 78.

[10] "The ALA Surveys Growth and Tastes in Reading," *Publishers' Weekly,* CLXXXI, No. 3 (January 15, 1962), 88.

[11] *Op. cit.*

tives, the community librarian can work as one of a community of inquirers.

No element in librarianship, if we shake off passivity and the custodial concept, can exist alone. The library that roots itself in the community will find rewards in sympathetic support and in a richer acquisition program.[12]

The public librarian must hold in central vision the total book situation in his community—the kinds of books provided in school, college, and public libraries. Service demarcations become artificial when the letter rather than the spirit guides policy. The public librarian should hold the overview, for he alone serves not one category of readers but all alike.

An integrating sense of the whole library, and of its relevance to the public, is possible to the community librarian as it cannot be to the huge book and information center. Ideally this sense could be reflected, in part at least, in a statement of book selection policy (which at the least should indorse the ALA "Freedom To Read" or "Bill of Rights" statement). Most of those I

have seen are very generalized. Let me quote, however, from that of the Oak Park, Illinois, Public Library, which has the virtues of concision and clarity:

> To enable citizens to form their own opinions, the library will attempt to provide materials that present all points of view. . . .
>
> A special attempt is made to collect books that are listed in standard library indexes, such as *Essay and General Literature Index* and *Granger's Index to Poetry and Recitations.*
>
> The selection of materials may be limited by the following factors: 1. The need for additional material in the existing collection; 2. The physical limitations of the building; 3. The suitability of the format of the material for library purposes; 4. Budgetary considerations; 5. Availability of specialized materials in more comprehensive library collections in the area.
>
> An up-to-date, attractive, and currently useful collection is maintained through a continual discarding and replacing process. . . .
>
> Experimental writing of high literary quality is given consideration since the public library assumes responsibility for collecting and encouraging writing that may influence the development of literature. . . .
>
> Books in such fields as medicine, psychology, and law that suggest procedures deemed harmful by recognized authorities will not be selected.[13]

---

[12] In her fine introductory—and re-introductory —guide to book selection, *Living with Books,* the late Helen E. Haines concluded her chapter, "Books for People," with a dozen points, the first five relating to library and community: "1. Study your community and know its general character, special characteristics, cultural and racial elements, chief activities, and leading interests. 2. Be familiar with subjects of present interest, general, national, and local. 3. Represent in book selection all subjects that apply to community conditions and that reflect community interests. 4. Make your collection of local history as extensive and useful as possible. 5. Provide for all organized groups whose activities or interests can be related to books." For the medium and smaller library, this further point: "Do not attempt to build up a 'complete' collection; select the best books on a subject, the best books of an author, the most useful volumes of a series, and do not make a fetish of 'full sets' that possess no specific and evident usefulness" (2d ed.; New York: Columbia University Press, 1950, p. 41).

[13] *Public Library Policies—General and Specific,* ed. Ruth M. White ("The Public Library Reporter," No. 9 [Chicago: American Library Association, 1960]), p. 17.

Of five "case-study" libraries analyzed by Dorothy Bendix, ranging from 15,000 to 80,000 in population and $40,000 to above $100,000 in income, none had a book selection policy statement, but two had adopted the "Library Bill of Rights" and one of these, in addition, had adopted the ALA "Freedom to Read" declaration. The case studies checked these, "considered the most crucial problems in public library book selection": "1. Quality standards . . . ; 2. Censorship; 3. Community characteristics and needs." There are somewhat inconclusive histories of procedure, allocation to specified types of purchase (disapproved, citing Helen Haines' opinion), standards, community pressures (Dorothy Bendix, "Some Problems in Book Selection Policies and Practices in Medium-Sized Public Libraries" [University of Illinois Library School *Occasional Papers,* No. 55, May, 1959]).

The notion of the open library, with meaningful interaction between book center and community, has only half emerged from the custodial chrysalis. If libraries are not built as community centers also, they ought to be; for responsive selection means an active and not a passive library and library program. The concerns of adult education participants, art- and foreign-film viewers, campers and garden and camera and union and woman's club, investment, Great Books and great discussions groups, can fire reader interest.

Our co-operation with the community college and Friends of the Library to present lecture series in the auditorium on modern art and on semantics stimulated interest and acquisition along these lines. Library book selection that does not take account of community enthusiasms, and that does not take a lead sometimes in some places to develop latent reading interest, has not begun to enter the new interpretive from the old custodial day.

To be related to community life, again, the library needs to grow more accessible in all its parts, from card catalog as finding guide rather than cataloger's crypt to reading areas designed to attract rather than repel the new reader. The outer walls are falling with passing of the architectural concept of the library as a monument. The inner fortress remains to be conquered.

Necessarily I speak of "ought," of a desirable tendency and direction. And remember, too, that for the library all activity external to the individual with a book has meaning only as it encourages the individual with a book.

The small community expands in meaning and resources as it looks out upon the greater community and to the issues that count most in the most humane and least partisan sense—that best define the current state of the "hominisation of man."

Emerson said in *The American Scholar:*

If there is any period one would desire to be born in, is it not the age of Revolution; when the old and the new stand side by side and admit of being compared; when the energies of all men are searched by fear and by hope; when the historic glories of the old can be compensated by the rich possibilities of the new era?

CURRENT AND LONG-RANGE ISSUES

Certainly we live in such a period. I want now, in my concluding comments, to underscore four current and long range issues that concern us as librarians and book selectors—now "when the energies of all men are searched by fear and by hope."

First, censorship. The Fiske study suggests that much censorship by libraries probably has been accomplished by librarians themselves, through rejection of potentially controversial books.[14] Rejection for social or political opinion or for manner of literary expression runs solidly against the ALA "Freedom To Read" statement, which asserts among other propositions: "It is in the public interest for publishers and librarians to make available the widest diversity of views and expressions, including those which are unorthodox or unpopular with the majority."

As the backbone for book selection policy, the "Freedom To Read" (Westchester) statement of ALA should be placed on the agenda of every library board and taken up for adoption point by point in a presentation by each librarian.

[14] M. Fiske, *Book Selection and Censorship* (Berkeley: University of California Press, 1959), p. 22.

Pressures have to be withstood because of the climate they can create. Last March several Iowa libraries rejected three Russian Embassy gift pamphlets containing information about the October, 1961, Soviet Communist Party Congress (much of it already printed in newspapers and magazines). This unwise rejection, drawing unfavorable and unflattering publicity, represented a desire—as in the Fiske study cases—to foreclose controversy. Freedom of the press and reporting and freedom to read cannot be disjoined. For both, the risk and the miracle of freedom are inseparable and in the creative American tradition.

Walter Lippmann argued in *The Indispensable Opposition* (back in 1939) that "if we truly wish to understand why freedom is necessary in a civilized society, we must begin by realizing that, because freedom of discussion improves our own opinions, the liberties of other men are our own vital necessity." Our own interest—the real if not always apparent interest of the community—is safeguarded, as well as the great democratic principle of tolerance, in resisting censorship. So, in the face of censorship for mode of literary expression, is another book selection principle: All books, like all adult experiences, are not necessarily for children.

Most libraries, I believe, need to interpret book selection policy more fully to their communities. And, since rejection is negative, they need also to be strong through positive selection in the sensitive areas most often affected by censorship.

The second issue concerns freshness and the longer view. Let us listen more than we generally do for new stirrings in our literature and life. *Booklist* and some other selection tools tend to con-

servatism; better late and cautious, they seem to say, than enthusiastic and unsure. Indications that poetry and painting have begun to rejoin the main currents of American life, from the byways of academic jargon and abstract expressionism, deserve our notice and sympathy. If we take a backward look at the books that were popular a century ago we shall perhaps be yet more inclined to listen for less well-known voices today. F. O. Matthiessen describes it in *American Renaissance:*

Whitman set up and printed *Leaves of Grass* for himself, and probably gave away more copies than were bought, whereas Longfellow could soon report (1857) that the total sales of his books had run to over three hundred thousand, and *Fern Leaves from Fanny's Portfolio* (1853) by the sister of N. P. Willis, sold a hundred thousand in its first year. Although *Typee* (1846) was more popular than Melville's subsequent work, it never came within miles of such figures. Hawthorne reported that six or seven hundred copies of *Twice-Told Tales* (1837) had been disposed of before the panic of that year descended.[15]

In *A Hope for Poetry,* written in 1934, Cecil Day-Lewis chose the ancestors for what was then the Auden Circle. Nowadays, of course, Auden has the same ancestors as everybody else, but the idea remains a good one and among the compensations which our profession, too, allows. "The brotherhood is not by the blood, certainly," MacLeish wrote. I nominate for inclusion among selected ancestors for library book selectors, among books already named here, Emerson's *The American Scholar* and Matthiessen's *American Renaissance.*

Sometimes new creative voices come in paper-bounds or magazines. Sometimes, more and more often, they challenge an old and long-held assumption

[15] Oxford: Oxford University Press, 1941, p. x.

—that American literature is but an extension of British literature, and they may remind us, if we grow disenchanted with some of what we see, that "The world is wide outside Verona's walls." The vigorous little magazine *The Sixties* (edited by Robert Bly at Odin House, Madison, Minnesota) does this in its Spring, 1962, issue in a pseudonymous article about the poet Gary Snyder, now living in a Japanese Buddhist monastery:

> In any case, Gary Snyder has displayed a courage of similar kind, not in order to face Whitman's devastating and perhaps unsurpassed criticism of America's puritanical materialism; but in order to undertake one of the tasks of the imagination for which Whitman often felt poets in America should prove most capable: the exploration of living traditions which, shunning the British tradition, nonetheless display powers of poetry which equal and sometimes surpass that tradition; and to make this search for the purpose of claiming America itself—by which I mean literally our own lives and the people and places we live among day by day—for the imagination [p. 40].

Once a teacher put it that the whole world is the patrimony of the whole world. In literature, increasingly, this can happen.

The third issue is desegregation. At the ALA national convention in 1962, some members of the ALA Council took the floor on behalf of moderation in library integration proceedings—an astounding spectacle in view of the fact that one hundred years after the Emancipation Proclamation the essence and hallmark of integration in our country is nothing else but moderation. Public access by all to the public library has no less significance than any other feature of desegregation, North *and* South. The burden of our stated belief, indeed, is that it holds a value unreckonably

high. Librarians have at least equal title to make it their own issue in terms commensurate with the value they place on libraries.

Emerson observed that great issues are not often tried on their merits but "the contention is ever hottest on minor matters." Desegregation of libraries is a great issue. Let us not have a great issue cut to lesser size.

The year 1963 marks the Emancipation Proclamation centennial. Why not National Library Week in 1963, and the general theme of library association activity, around Library Freedom, including both issues of desegregation and censorship? This would give more positive content to National Library Week—something needed to break the high level of abstraction of its publicity—and involve libraries in issues of book and community concern.

A fourth and final issue. The public library with its shelves open to all varieties of opinion and to many different images of the human future ought to look with special sympathy at the United Nations and its late secretary-general, described by Joseph Lash in *Dag Hammarskjold, Custodian of the Brushfire Peace* as the first great exemplar and martyr for "The International Priesthood." A devoted reader, Hammarskjold spoke of his insistence upon reading at least an hour each evening, no matter how arduous the day, as "a necessary mental exercise." During the Suez crisis he remarked: "Listening to Bach's Sixth Brandenburg Concerto, in a way, is like reading an extremely good book or poem." No better tribute could have been devised—and none more meaningful for librarians—than the dedication to Hammarskjold of the United Nations Library.

If, serving the smaller community, we open passage to the great community, we shall play our part in an event of startling beauty. It will come at the close of our race's planet-bound infancy and the early light of a new space-oriented morning. For the first time during the troubled long legend of people on the earth a rainbow, world-wide, imaginative book will open for all the world, no myth remote or art strange in its glow, no child too dark or too fair to enter any public library and see.

The library's highest calling now is to be a microcosm of the coming united states of man, representing as it should all times and places and creative voices. Let us as librarians prove active legislators in our republic of free communion and communication; and equally, at the same time, preservers of the American tradition founded in humane experiment, who know and say that such a republic could not exist under authoritarian government of either Left or Right. Let us be interpreters for the redeeming ministry of books.

PROBLEMS OF LIBRARY CONSTRUCTION

RALPH A. ULVELING

THE planning of a new library building or a major enlargement of an existing library is a project of such dimensions that the institutional investment involved will likely not be repeated for half a century or more. Most librarians who are confronted with such a problem have had no experience to prepare them for it. They may have attended one or more ALA building institutes, and they probably have heard a few lectures on building planning as part of an administration course in library school years before. These are a helpful introduction to planning, but sometimes they give a false sense of security to both the librarians and their governing boards. These same boards and librarians would recognize at once the folly of allowing someone with such a very meager background to assume the responsibility for cataloging the library's books. I point to this incongruity even though it must be obvious to all that cataloging errors would lend themselves to easy correction in a way that a building error would not.

Today, a library board confronted with a new building project would probably engage the services of a library building consultant, just as school administrators turn to school consultants, hospital administrators to hospital consultants, and industrialists to factory layout consultants. Wheeler and Githens have written:

The planning of a library is an intricate matter. It is too much to expect anyone, in the few months while a library plan takes shape, to master the intricacies of a complex and rapidly developing subject in which only a few architects and librarians are fairly competent after a lifetime of study and practice. Most businessmen agree that technical advisors are well worth the cost. It is an evidence of good judgment and no reflection on the intelligence of trustees to call in an experienced advisor before starting sketch plans, thus preventing unnecessary expense, inefficient service, and lasting regret.[1]

That statement was made more than two decades ago. However, in a recent issue of the *Library Journal,* we find new evidence of the failure of a librarian and architect to comprehend fully the ideas of one another. In that issue a prominent architect of White Plains, New York, said:

Where the library director and the architect present as differing a report on one aspect of the library planning as we find here, there has obviously been a failure in communication somewhere along the line. . . . The language of an architect in communicating his designs to others must remain basically the language of his drawings. To most who are laymen in respect to architecture and building, this is a foreign language to greater or less degree.[2]

It is true, unfortunately, that many laymen who profess the ability to read architectural plans see them in two dimensions only. They often fail to see differences in elevation. Yet, it is the height of objects, such as freestanding shelving or other visual obstructions, as well as variations in floor levels, etc., that can create real operating difficul-

[1] J. L. Wheeler and A. M. Githens, *The American Public Library Building* (New York: Charles Scribner's Sons, 1941), p. 59.

[2] W. H. Heidtmann, "Haste and Misunderstanding," *Library Journal,* LXXXVII, No. 9 (May 1, 1962), 1718.

ties and deep-seated disappointments for the librarian and the board.

In general, a good library consultant can be expected to do many things: (*a*) aid in clarifying the library's service requirements, being sure to bring up for consideration services, or methods, or programs that may have been overlooked but that should be considered; (*b*) translate the library's needs into terms that can be readily grasped by the architect; (*c*) clarify for the librarian and board the architectural limitations that must be recognized in developing a plan; (*d*) confer with the librarian and architect—first in developing and then in refining the building plans; and (*e*) give guidance and counsel to the librarian and board on all problems that may be related to the building project. I emphasize the words "guidance and counsel" simply because there are some things no building consultant can be expected to do, such as convincing city officials or the townspeople of the need to provide funds for a new library building. Nor can a building consultant work out the interior decoration and furnishing of the building, though this is often expected. However, in both of these matters and in many similar ones, his broad experience will make it possible for him to give knowledgeable advice.

With this background let us consider the three phases of a building project: the preliminary planning of the services and methods; the principles to follow in building layout; and the creation of the plan.

PRELIMINARY PLANNING OF THE SERVICES AND METHODS

The time to begin modernizing operating methods and planning new services is *before* rather than *after* the building plans are drawn. It is not unusual to hear librarians say: "After we get into the new building, the next thing we are going to do is investigate various charging and registration systems with a view to modernizing ours. Right now we are so busy we can't think about such things." That is the wrong time to do it. Why provide the space for a mass of slip trays and registration files if a year after going into a new building all the processes are to be streamlined? It has happened that the useless space thus provided at considerable extra expense actually militates against whatever compact plan may be instituted.

Similarly *new* services to be added should be anticipated before even schematic plans are prepared. Will the library have a collection of circulating sound recordings? If so, ample space for examining each recording at the charge-out and return desks must be provided and a place for listening equipment and special shelving must be included in one of the rooms. If a film service is to be maintained, a place for checking, repairing, and cleaning the films will be essential. Some provision for previewing the films, either by the staff, the public, or both, must be made. Will the book collection be continued as one central collection or will one or more special departments be created? Regardless of the number of administrative offices required currently, in a growing community it is likely that more will be needed before long. Provide space now which can later be divided by movable partitions.

Likewise, prepare the best estimates you can make of the size of the book collection to be housed eventually, with separate figures for the adult and juvenile collections; the number of periodicals that will be received currently; the number of seats to be provided in each department; the number of persons you feel is the maximum to be seated in the meeting room at one time; and the number of staff members for whom provision should be made. The latter figure should be divided into male and female, so that lavatory and locker spaces may be anticipated. Through the years the proportion of one sex to another will change; the quarters for each should provide leeway.

These are the facts and figures that any librarian should have before a consultant is brought in. The figures may be revised in the course of discussion with the consultant. But since no two libraries are exactly alike, and since no two library programs are identical, it is basic that the ideas and the plans of the local administration be the starting point for all that follows.

PRINCIPLES TO FOLLOW IN BUILDING LAYOUTS

John Burchard, architect-librarian-educator, once said: "Librarians, like cooks, know what they do but not *why* they do it nor *how* they could do it better."[3] This is not a very flattering statement and one which surely does not apply to services, though it may to building considerations. In any case, I shall try to state some principles to consider in planning a building.

1. *Patrons can be moved horizontally more easily than vertically and with greater safety and economy.* Ideally then, public services should, if possible, be kept on one floor—the ground floor.

[3] Quoted in C. M. Mohrhardt and R. A. Ulveling, "Public Libraries," *Architectural Record* ("Building Types," Study No. 193) CXII (December, 1952), 150.

This, of course, is not even possible, or desirable, for libraries that have become quite large. Availability of land for sites also affects the extent to which a library can apply this principle.

From a cost standpoint, I point out that if only one public department is moved off the ground floor, that fact may entail a building expense out of all proportion to the size of the service area required. Local building safety regulations almost uniformly would require two stair exits from an upstairs or a basement public room. If a stairwell occupies a minimum of 125 square feet on one floor, it will require a total of 250 square feet on two floors. Double that for two stairwells and you find that at $20 per square foot (I am using this figure for explanatory purposes only) you are spending $10,000 just to get to the other level. For that much money you could have had a very significant enlargement for one of the main-floor departments.

2. To provide the maximum future flexibility for the library, *keep all unmovable building features in one area instead of being scattered through the building.* I am referring to such items as stairways, elevators, toilets, etc. Avoid built-in seats, desks, decorative borders in floors around book stacks or other designated areas. Fixed elements such as these tend to freeze the plan and make the building less flexible to meet future needs.

Librarians, too, must control what seems to be a group characteristic—that of wanting to separate each different kind of activity by a wall. For example, instead of a built-in closet for supplies, use a free-standing supply cabinet. This has many advantages: it saves the cost of the closet walls and door; it permits the supply space to be enlarged later; and it permits the supply space to be moved to another location. You may be surprised to learn that the amount of space occupied by walls is often as much as 10 per cent of the total floor area. Further, walls not only reduce the aggregate available space within a building, but they lessen the usability of the areas that remain. Open spaces can be used far more efficiently than space divided into smaller parcels.

3. *As far as possible, strive to make things serve two purposes instead of one.* Toilet rooms can often be so located as to be readily accessible to readers using the library and also available to the audience using the meeting room after the library proper has closed. In locating toilets, however, place them where the entrances can be supervised during the time the library is open for general service. A story-hour room used only for a weekly story hour is a luxury few libraries can afford. Such a room, however, should be so placed as to have direct easy access from both the children's and the adult areas; it may serve as a meeting room for people of various ages. The corollary to this is that the room should not be decorated in a fairy tale or similarly childish motif. It is quite possible to develop an interesting decor that will be equally appropriate for adults and for children.

A single workroom placed between two departments where it can be shared will be less costly to build than two separate workrooms. A jointly used workroom will also permit operating economies. For example, one typewriter and one typist may be all that are necessary, whereas two separate workrooms would almost surely necessitate the purchase of two typewriters and possibly would necessitate duplication of typists.

4. One subject that might have been included under shared facilities is so important that it demands separate mention. I refer to the question of *whether or not children's books should be charged at the library's general control desk or in the children's room.* In the light of a long and extensive experience in library consulting, I believe I can say that nothing is more hotly championed one way or the other, and that nothing is farther from reaching a commonly accepted solution. Some children's librarians resent the idea that children should come through a separate door and be treated any differently than any other person. They imply, without putting it into words, that anyone who supports another position just "hasn't seen the light." Those who champion separate charging arrangements for children seem to think that someone who knows children's books must pass on the book being taken by each little patron lest he get something unsuitable for him or her. I feel that this position is untenable, simply because it seems to me that any supervision or help in selecting reading matter should be given *before* the child makes his choice rather than after. I have not attempted to assemble comparative figures, but I have a feeling that the number who favor having all children's books charged by clerks at the general control desk is now numerically larger and that that group will eventually become dominant.

5. A principle that requires repeated enunciation is to *avoid emulating special building features of other types of institutions* unless they can logically be

defended as sound for libraries. I believe the somewhat popular conception that public libraries should have drive-up windows like the progressive new banks is fallacious. Book drops for the return of books is an unquestioned service to the borrower. But these require no more than a slit in the wall or door, certainly not a window with an attendant. The patron's relationship to a bank is altogether different from that of his relationship to a library. I know of no place where the patron is so completely independent of the need for consultation as in his normal banking activities. Either he will deposit money, cash checks, or withdraw money. He alone can make these decisions. The patron in these cases needs no counsel from the banker. But if he does need counsel, either on investments or the taking out of a mortgage or on anything more than the deposit or withdrawal of money, he would never attempt to get it at a drive-up window. He would park his car and go in. Likewise, he would go into a store to select the merchandise he wants. And the store with its big array of products on display surely would not feel it was sensible, as a business practice, to make it possible for customers to remain in their automobiles while on a buying expedition. Similarly, libraries that are concerned with guiding readers in a meaningful way would not be content to restrict their contact with patrons to a short telephone message followed later by passing a package of books through a window. Much could be said, too, of the unsound economics of this kind of service procedure, but I do not wish to attach undue importance to it here. Suffice it to say that libraries do not enhance their service or their standing in the community by adopting the ill-fitting ways of other organizations. People believe, and rightfully so, that librarians are quite capable of devising sound, progressive practices for their institutions, and that they will provide normal new conveniences as was done when drop boxes and book-return slots were taken up widely. Artificial copying of others is neither necessary nor desirable.

6. Another principle I wish to recommend is to *leave some space "unassigned"* in any new building. Developments are coming so fast that the little leeway thus provided is frequently used up before the building is three years old. It is not wasteful; it is good sense to recognize openly that the building under construction must provide for more than today's requirements.

7. Finally, I turn to a very controversial matter—the location of the library site. If the decision has been made to rebuild on the old library site, then what follows will have no bearing on your problem. However, if the existing library lot is too small, or too poorly located to serve successfully for a new building, choices will have to be considered. *Do not follow outdated principles in choosing a library site.*

A quarter-century or more ago, the principle was laid down and broadly accepted that a library should be at the main intersection of the downtown area. We have learned much since that time, but even more significant is the fact that our social patterns nationally have changed. However, no one to my knowledge has challenged the appropriateness of that dictum for today's conditions, as I do now. During the Hoover administration, we were much aware of a popular slogan that referred to a chicken in every pot and a car in every garage. That was used to suggest the optimum in abundance. Today, even in the homes of quite modest salaried workers, it is becoming common to find a car for every worker. A man and wife each holding jobs may well have two cars. Grown sons and daughters in a household increase the need for, and the number of, cars. This has resulted in a kind of population mobility that has brought on the growth of great outlying shopping centers, suburban living, the threatened collapse of good public transportation, and the downgrading in importance of the downtown areas of cities generally. In Detroit and in hundreds of communities, the busiest corner is no longer a downtown intersection but a place miles and miles out from the city center where automobiles by the thousands pass every hour. I am not saying that the library must be located remote from the downtown area. I am merely decrying acceptance of the slick, easily mouthed formula of earlier years that the main intersection downtown is the ideal site for a main library. Each city must be analyzed as a separate problem. The close proximity of large municipal parking lots may be far more important in choosing a library site than other factors.

I am sure that all of you are well aware of the frustration of trying to find a place to leave an automobile while you go into a bank, a post office, or any other similar building. I am sure, too, that you have found it far easier to pass your usual drug store and drive a mile beyond to another if you are assured of a parking space when you get there. There is nothing compulsive about using a library. If you have difficulty finding a place to park your car

every time you go, or if parking fees are unreasonable in commercial parking grounds near the library, you will gradually forego frequent trips to it, and so will others. Parking is not the only factor to be considered in site selection, but be sure to consider it when you locate your building, and do not be guided by principles that may have been good in the 1930's but are now no longer valid.

CREATION OF THE PLAN

As you approach the actual work of getting your hopes on paper in definite realizable form, of necessity you create a planning team. The care and judgment applied in developing that team will largely determine the results you obtain. The librarian, the architect, and the building consultant will each have a principal part in the undertaking. A fourth member—the interior designer —will be discussed later. The building consultant is to see that a sound functional plan is devised, one which will adequately meet the service needs the library is to provide for. The architect is to develop a suitable and pleasing form for housing the activity. Neither of these should trespass on the field of the other and usually they do not. The librarian represents the owner and, as such, is in position to veto the proposals of either of the other two members if those proposals seem unsuitable for the community. He must, however, remain open-minded and receptive to suggestions.

"The best consultant," says a prominent North Carolina architect, "is an experienced administrator in the particular field for which a building is being planned. If neither the architect nor the client is familiar with the problems inherent to a building of highly specialized use, such as a library, then in lieu of research by the architect and owner a consultant would be desirable. ... I treasure the recollection of Charles Mohrhardt's performance when the planning of the Winston-Salem Public Library was bogging down in a confusion of professional and amateur advice. After studying overnight the proposed plans, which were in advanced working drawing stage, Mr. Mohrhardt [who had just been called into consultation at that point in the library's planning] recommended a completely new approach. His reasons were sound and convincing. His advice was followed."[4]

HOW TO CHOOSE A CONSULTANT

Since the term "consultant" has many applications, a few words on the selection of a consultant may be in order. Two points of possible confusion need clarification: (1) Eminence in the library profession is not synonomous with experience in planning buildings. Not infrequently, however, one will hear a board speak of engaging some librarian of a nearby city to guide its building project. The choice is sometimes made for no better reason than that the librarian is close at hand and is well known in the state. (2) Similarly, the consultants from the state library who periodically tour the state are for the most part service and operational advisors, not building experts. They fill a very important function but that function must be recognized for what it is.

Before discussing the kind of serv-

ices various consultants provide, it is necessary to define some commonly used terms that may be misunderstood unless the trade use of the terms is known.

The *building program* is usually a written statement of the philosophy, principles, requirements, and limitations that are prepared to guide the architect. (Some library building consultants limit their services largely to preparation of the building program.)

Schematic plans are proposed floor layouts that have been developed in the light of all the requirements that have been given. They represent a possible solution for the problem that is set up in the building program. Sometimes several schematic plans must be prepared. When one plan is acceptable, it will be used as the basis for the preliminary plans.

Preliminary plans, though based on the approved schematic plan, are developed by the architect in much greater detail. These plans show the location and space requirements for everything to be contained in the building, including the structural building requirements. The preliminary plans together with an *outline of specifications* prepared by the architect provide the basis for preparing a preliminary cost estimate for the entire structure.

Working drawings together with *specifications* are the detailed contract documents used by builders for the preparation of bids and for erection of the building. Working drawings include elevations, sections, and details. Further, these drawings show architectural, structural, and mechanical work.

Specifications include a written description of the scope of the work, general conditions, the materials to be

[4] L. Lashmit, "The Architect's Function in Preliminary Planning," *Proceedings of the Institute sponsored by the American Library Association Buildings Committee* (Chicago: American Library Association, 1954), p. 16.

used, and the workmanship involved in the project.

Shop drawings are drawings of details prepared by the fabricator of special features of the building. These are done for the contractor at no added expense to the library. They must be submitted to the architect for his approval before the work can go forward.

Thus, in selecting the consultant, find out in what form his reports will be presented—as a written building program that in effect defines the problem, or as a schematic drawing with accompanying explanatory reports, which are proposed solutions to the building problem. The latter, which are more difficult to prepare, are usually more readily understood by the librarian and the board and they convey to the architect a more definite conception of what will be needed. (A word of warning, however, should be included here. Architects usually welcome a well-prepared schematic plan, but they become annoyed when confronted with a proposed scheme that is an amateurish hodgepodge of rooms stuck together without the discipline of a controlled plan.)

Also, you should get a record of the consulting work he has done in the past. Examine this as to extent and variety. Visit some of the libraries referred to, if possible. Find out from the librarian of one of these buildings how well the consultant works with the board and with the architect. One librarian made a somewhat more thorough analysis of the work of various consultants and found out that the actual building costs per square foot for one consultant were usually less than for others, regardless of which architectural firm he worked with.

Further, make sure that your consultant will not consider his responsibility ended when he presents a typed report for handing to an architect. A fully satisfying consultant will not disassociate himself from the project until the building is occupied. Weigh all these factors and then make your selection.

WHEN SHOULD A CONSULTANT BE BROUGHT IN?

The first person to be added to your building team should be the building consultant. This should be done long before an architect is engaged. The time for this is when the librarian and board begin serious consideration of a building project. Very often this is before the financing of a new building has been provided—when the board is often uncertain about what moves to make. Should the present building be enlarged? Would a small branch relieve the main library sufficiently? Or should someone do an over-all library survey and in that way find out just what should be done about the building? Let me speak briefly of each of these points, beginning with the last:

1. A general library survey may be needed to get some appraisal of its services, its operating methods, the quality and extent of its book collection. But if it is recognized that a more adequate building is needed, a survey is usually only an instrument for deferring the coming to grips with a decision that sooner or later must be made.

2. A branch library or many branch libraries will duplicate in part some of the service of the main library and thus make these services available to more people more conveniently. But it will very seldom diminish the pressures at the main library sufficiently to affect that library's building requirements.

The raised educational level of people throughout this country, the growth of reading interests both in breadth and especially in depth or specialization, require far bigger, broader, and better main libraries everywhere. A branch can to an extent relieve the student load but, except in the case of large branch libraries (larger than I have envisioned for the cities under consideration), it cannot provide the range of reading matter demanded by an educated adult clientele.

3. Should the present building be enlarged? Though each building presents a unique problem, some generalizations can be made. An amazing number of libraries in medium-sized cities are in Carnegie buildings that were erected fifty or more years ago, when the communities they serve were far smaller. Most of these buildings are literally unsuitable for major expansion. The basements usually have a veritable forest of supporting columns, thus making it completely impossible to assemble enough open area at that level to locate a service. Many of these early buildings have already had additions so badly planned and placed that all possibility of further expansion is precluded. Nearly all have the main service area far above the ground level, thus making it difficult or even impossible for many elderly people and people with heart ailments to use the library. And frequently the service areas of these buildings are so difficult to integrate into a unified, open plan that operating costs will inevitably be higher than would be necessary in a better organized structure. An over-all admonition then would be: Do not be misled by the fact that the present building is in excellent physical condition. Uniformly, such buildings have been so well maintained and are nearly always so monumental in design that a serious resistance can develop to any proposals concerning replacement. Usually, however, when sentiment has forced the retention of the existing building, the over-all construction costs have been nearly as large as if an entirely new building had been erected. And often the operating cost for staffing is larger.

The last member of the planning team—the interior designer—may be unfamiliar to many. I begin my comment by warning that interior designers resent being confused with interior decorators. The basic difference, I believe, is in the scope of the work which each is prepared to handle. I have heard, too, that there is a fundamental difference in the amount and kind of training of each; I cite this only as hearsay, for I have no intention of making myself the target of a controversy on this point. The interior decorator is concerned with adding equipment and color to a completed building. The interior designer is concerned not only with all equipment and color but, further, with the choice of materials for floors and walls, with lighting equipment, and with all those building features that become a part of the total symphony of parts in a finished room.

One of his great strengths is that he is competent and often very ingenious in suggesting or even designing new kinds of special equipment to meet special needs. Many architects like to control all the finish detail for their buildings, and some of the very large architectural firms, therefore, maintain interior-design departments within their own organizations. Many other architects are very happy to work with any recognized interior designer. Be certain, however, that the interior designer you engage is not representing one single manufacturer and that he is free and ready to draw from the products of all and is in the employ of none.

My advice regarding the final phase of your building project would be to avail yourself of the services of a competent interior designer. If you wish your building to have a smart appearance as opposed to the look of an amateur decorator, I strongly urge you not to rely on any staff member, even though one may have a reputation for being very clever in handling colors. A good librarian has neither the time nor the opportunity to keep up with all the new thinking and new developments in a field so unrelated to our own.

HOW MUCH MONEY SHOULD BE REQUESTED FROM THE CITY?

I begin this section by saying that the standard indexes of construction costs —the engineering News-Record Building Cost Index and the Building Commodity Index—show that these costs have been rising steadily and sharply since 1950 or before. This, plus the fact that people have a natural inclination to allow their desires to influence their judgment when estimating prices, results in some early surprises on probable costs for a building. Some board member, at this point in the planning, is quite likely to say: "This is a very conservative community." In other words, cut the price. But a board must be realistic. If the schools and other local interests pay standard rates for construction, the library will have to do so, too. The building rates cannot be cut. And if the estimates of the library's needs were correct, they can be cut only a very little.

Because the consultant has a degree of detachment not enjoyed by the members of the board who have the responsibility for providing the needed funds, he can sometimes be helpful in giving general counsel. I remember one board that was quite perturbed to learn that the building they wanted would cost about $500,000. Gradually, conversation led around to a proposal that "we ask for $350,000 which is the figure we discussed a year ago." Their attitude changed, however, when it was pointed out that as a board they have a responsibility to tell the community the facts as they know them. Otherwise, if it should become known that the new building is inadequate and the board knew it would be at the time it was planned, the people will feel that the library board was incompetent and irresponsible. On the other hand, if the board stated the true needs and then the city fathers or the townspeople allowed only a lesser amount, the good faith and the confidence of all would have been preserved. There is real danger in altering any facts merely to make them palatable. Amazingly, too, most communities, once they pass the point of early surprise, are willing to provide for all reasonable needs for the library just as they do for the schools.

CONCLUDING STATEMENT

A well-planned building not only provides for all needs of readers and staff but has a simplicity of layout that permits patrons, even on their first visit, to grasp easily the service plan. It is difficult to devise a plan in which services are so located that each may function with the least interference possible from the users of other services in the building. It is difficult, too, to arrange a layout that gives the maximum access by all departments to the library resources they will need and to do this while making it possible to supervise the building with a minimum of staff. In short, it is difficult and time-consuming to devise a satisfactory, functional, appealing plan that is also a simple plan. For this reason allow plenty of time in the early stages both for creating a plan and then for studying it. It is a relatively small matter to remove a wall on a drawing by means of an eraser. But once the wall is built, its removal is not so simple. Changes in a plan that are made after a construction contract has been awarded also create complications and will necessitate "change orders." Such late changes are expensive, and often they affect more separate trades working on the building than most laymen realize. Avoid them by disciplining your early eagerness to get the work going. Control that very strong urge to get the digging started before the project has been fully matured in the planning stage. The dividends for early patience are large.

NEW TECHNOLOGY: PROMISE AND REALITY

HERBERT GOLDHOR

I<small>T</small> IS not difficult to accept the assumption expressed by the conveners of this conference that public libraries serving from 25,000 to 150,000 people will long continue to be with us. Indeed, they undoubtedly will grow in number and importance, both by virtue of their own natural growth—and it is in this size group that the greatest percentage of population growth is occurring—and as a result of the consolidation of even smaller library units. As communities grow in size from the lower limit of this medium-sized group to the upper limit, their public libraries increase on the average from five to six times in various possible measures of scope of operations, or more than in any other population grouping. This group of libraries is indeed the middle group between those surely large enough for effective and efficient operation and those surely too small in general to provide adequate public library service.

This in-between state of these medium-sized public libraries is especially critical in regard to the use of machinery and technological developments. Limited budgets, limited staff, and limited know-how all combine to make a vicious circle. For the hard truth is that most public libraries of this group do not make as much use of machines as is made in the average modern house. This statement is made without documentation but in full confidence of its accuracy. If you will add up in your mind the number of different electric motors in your own home, I predict you will find you have twenty or more. The average public library in this size group has less than that. Not that electric motors are the only desirable kinds of machines in libraries, but most machines and technological developments require a mechanical source of energy, and the small electric motor is the best source of such power now in use.

It is easy and safe, therefore, to predict that libraries of this size are sure to add more motors and more machines in the years ahead.[1] This is not to say that it is always wise to do so, as I hope to show in specific ways soon. But on the whole there has been not enough emphasis rather than too much on the desirable use of machines in libraries. Librarians are too prone to favor hand methods, to insist on numerous exceptions and special treatment, to resist change, to deprecate new methods that shift the burden (or even some of the burden) onto the patron, and actually to resist even those machines that are quite ordinary. And to aid and abet these feelings there are figures that can be cited showing that hand methods are as fast as or faster than machines, and

[1] Good general references to the use of machines in libraries are R. Blasingame, "Punched Cards," Part 3, Vol. 4 of Ralph R. Shaw (ed.), *The State of the Library Art* (New Brunswick, N.J.: Rutgers University Graduate School of Library Service, 1961), pp. 101–36; M. M. Berry, "Application of Punched Cards to Library Routines," in Robert S. Casey *et al.* (eds.), *Punched Cards: Their Applications to Science and Industry* (2d ed.; New York: Reinhold Publishing Corp., 1958), pp. 279–302; and A. H. Trotier (ed.), "Mechanization in Libraries," *Library Trends*, V (October, 1956), 191–308.

cost less. But you will notice that few business houses use the abacus—though it too has been shown to be superior to a calculating machine! The point is, of course, that skilled abacus operators are able to outperform an electric calculator, but the calculator can be effectively used by a far-from-skilled operator and will never get tired (though it will have breakdowns) and will never ask for a vacation or more pay or a maternity leave.

Three main considerations should determine any library's acquisition of a machine. First, can it do a job that is needed and do it at least reasonably well, reasonably fast, and reasonably cheap? Second, is it capable of some flexibility in handling new jobs and changes in these jobs? Third, and most important, is it likely to be able to handle an increased workload up to at least double what is now involved? The long-term shortage of manpower and the increasing cost of salaries and fringe benefits, plus the inevitable growth and expansion to be expected by most American public libraries of this size group, all make it desirable to judge machines by their value in handling that ever larger workload (sure to come in the foreseeable future) with no appreciable increase in staff.

PHYSICAL PLANT

There are at least three main areas for the application of machines and technological improvements in libraries: the physical plant, office and service routines, and technical and professional operations. In the realm of physical plant, I refer to such things as modern heating and air-conditioning, power tools, floor-cleaning machines, etc. Heating a library building today should certainly involve a fuel such as natural gas or oil, and thermostats to provide zone control. Electronic filters for removing dust and dirt from the air are now available in packaged units for the home, and at least one small public library (at Dover, Ohio) is known to have them. Air-conditioning in any part of our country is now as necessary in a public library as is heating, and is as necessary and desirable in a public library as in a private home or in a salesroom.

To be sure, these devices are easier to include when erecting a new building than to add to an existing building, but they are not impossible or even difficult to add, and they are not very expensive. I would estimate that the cost of converting to an automatic heating system in a library building would be recovered in about five years by the saving in direct cost of janitorial labor needed to shovel coal or to feed and tend a stoker system.

Power tools have revolutionized the building industry in the last twenty years, but I wonder how many medium-sized public libraries have a power saw, a belt sander, a planer, or a paint-sprayer. Yet these cost about $250 altogether, and are essential to a carpenter attempting to keep a building in repair and might even be used to construct or refinish furniture. Of course, it is equally necessary to have a custodian who is able to use such tools, but such men are available and at a reasonable salary (especially if they do not have to spend most of their time feeding a furnace). This is a small illustration of the general truth that technology creates new opportunities by changing the character of the requisite duties.

An even more mundane example of

the available machines that libraries will surely utilize increasingly is to be found in the equipment for cleaning floors. A scrubber-polisher is fairly standard for all institutions in this size group. Less common perhaps but even more helpful is the wet pick-up machine that in effect replaces the mop bucket and wringer. Together, these machines will wash and scrub a floor and pick up the dirty water; and they cost about $700. This illusrates a second great truth about the impact of technology—it often serves to lift the burden of work from people's backs.

Other possible devices in this general area would include elevators, automotive equipment (especially bookmobiles with their own power generators), intercommunication devices, timer clocks to turn electric current on or off, electric-eye door openers, and many other items common in the modern world. Some of them are more appropriate to larger libraries, but the long-term trend is for them to be used more and more by smaller libraries. All the devices are being improved steadily, and the price of most of them is reasonable even for a medium-sized public library when we consider the benefits they bring.

OFFICE AND SERVICE ROUTINES

The world of business and office machines also offers many possible applications. Few of us realize the tremendous advances that have been made in office equipment. Take the humble typewriter, for example, which at one time came in one model with at most a few optional special characters and a choice between pica and elite type. Today, of course, there are both standard desk and portable models, manual or electric, with a wide variety of type faces—indeed, it is possible to use more than one

type face on the same machine—and many optional characters. Typewriters come with either a cloth ribbon or a carbon ribbon (the latter much to be preferred for copy to be photographed) or both. Some typewriters have proportional spacing (so that the letter m takes proportionately more space than the letter i). In two typings they can prepare an evenly spaced line to fit a justified right-hand margin. Platens may be standard or wide. These do not exhaust the possible features.[2]

All that is needed, one might say, is a machine that will type by itself. Exactly so, and there are at least four well-known makes that offer automatic typewriters, actuated by punched cards, punched tape, or punched rolls of paper much like the old player-piano rolls. These automatic typewriters operate at speeds of one hundred words per minute and are especially useful in preparing a number of copies of a document when each needs to be an original. They can be programmed to a greater or lesser degree to omit or include different items or paragraphs in different copies, and have been used successfully in several libraries to reproduce catalog cards.[3] To be sure, such a typewriter

[2] "Tools of the Office: Typewriters," *Office Management and American Business,* XXII (January, 1961), 108, 110, 112.

[3] F. J. Witty, "The Flexowriter and Catalog Card Reproduction: Perfect Solution for Short Runs?" *DC Libraries,* XXVIII (July, 1957), 2–4; G. R. Luckett, "Partial Library Automation with the Flexowriter Automatic Writing Machine," *Library Resources and Technical Services,* I (Fall, 1957), 207–10; H. H. Bernstein, "The Use of Flexowriters in Documentation Centers and Libraries," *UNESCO Bulletin for Libraries,* XVI (March–April, 1962), 79–85; L. A. Kenney, "New Card Making Equipment at State Library," *Illinois Libraries,* XLI (June, 1959), 417–20; A. Nylund, "Catalog Workload Diminished," *Pioneer,* XXII (December, 1959), 6–7; and de Lafayette Reid, "Automatic Catalog Card Processing," *Pioneer,* XXIII (March–April, 1960), 4–5.

costs about $2,500, but if it saves even ten hours' time a week of a typist, it will pay for itself in four years.

Another example of the great improvements in office machines is to be found in the various devices for printing: for example, the hectograph, the Mimeograph, and the multilith. These range in price from about $100 to $1,000, but no medium-sized public library should be without one or more. For about $500 you can buy an electric Mimeograph that takes a ream of paper at a time, can be set to stop after producing a designated number of copies, uses waterbase ink that will not smear or rub off, can print in colors, utilizes plates with etched-on pictures, and produces several thousand copies from a single stencil. Again, as with the power tools for the custodian, these machines are of little value without people able and skilled in using them. But modern business schools teach their students the use of many of these machines, and any efficient equipment company will train a library's own employees in the use of its products when you buy them.

Not only are most business machines being developed into ever more useful and flexible devices, but there are more such machines available than most medium-sized public libraries have discovered or are using. Among these are machines to fold paper (useful in preparing book lists, annual reports or other publicity), tape calculators (which perform all four arithmetical operations and produce a complete printed record), and motorized rotary card cabinets.

Some general-purpose machines particularly useful in libraries include the Potdevin edge-gluer for applying date due slips or plastic book jackets; the Seal dry-mounting press for mounting pictures and for other purposes; tape, disks, or wire recorders for dictating letters, charging books for loan, or answering the telephone when the library is closed; and addressing machines (used either as such or to reproduce catalog cards). Some machines of a specialized nature are also of natural use in libraries: for example, motion picture projectors (not to speak of electric rewinds), phonograph record turntables, and automatic slide projectors.

Photographic devices deserve particular notice. Most medium-sized public libraries should have a microfilm reading machine, and should arrange for the microfilming of the local newspaper if that has not already been done. This is most desirable, both from the point of view of the saving of space and the longer life of film than of newsprint. In addition, there are newspapers of national importance available on film, as well as many journals and other special items. Next in importance to a microfilm reader is a reader-printer which within seconds gives a lifesize reproduction of the microfilm. At least two well-known makes are now available. A microfilm camera is used in one of the more popular new systems of circulation control, and has an often unsuspected use in filming those business records of the library that need to be preserved. Every library of this size group should have an office photocopying device. These are available in many different makes and models, and the best give a clear copy in a few minutes at a low cost and with a minimum of processing. For library purposes, secure one that can copy pages from a bound volume as well as loose sheets. It is evident that medium-sized public libraries will utilize such machines ever more in the years ahead.

TECHNICAL AND PROFESSIONAL
OPERATIONS

We come now to what is obviously the most important potential application of modern technology to libraries —the use of punched cards such as are handled by IBM or Remington Rand machines. This is no longer a dream or a distant reality. At least a dozen American libraries (including some medium-sized public libraries) have had up to twenty years of experience with fairly complicated machine installations. It is as easy and safe to predict that such machines will play an ever more important role in the future of medium-sized public libraries as it was to foresee greatly increased use of machines in physical plant and in office work.

Machine-punched cards are of use to public libraries in at least three main areas: business office procedures, circulation control, and book-ordering and cataloging. Library applications of punched cards to financial records, personnel data, and other such purposes are not essentially different from similar situations in the business world, except that the volume is so low in most public libraries as to make it unprofitable and uneconomic to use a machine system for these purposes alone.

In circulation control, on the other hand, libraries have a high volume of repetitive operations. Medium-sized public libraries as here defined will have an annual total circulation of about 150,000 to 1,000,000 or more. Any public library using a circulation system today that requires slipping or discharging of books is less efficient than if it were to adopt one of the several different systems that eliminate this step. Most but not all of these systems require a serially numbered transaction card, and machine-punched *t*-cards are relatively inexpensive to buy, sort, and maintain. A small keypunch and an electric sorter rent for about $50 a month. Actually there are even better circulation systems that are even more different from the traditional hand methods, such as the Wayne County system of disposable *t*-cards and the McColvin token system of charging. But for a library that has punched-card equipment or that is interested in the use of punched cards for other purposes, any of the photographic or audio charging systems employing punched transaction cards can be recommended.

The third main application of punched cards to public library operations is in the field of book ordering, cataloging, and related use of bibliographic data. The essential principle involved is simply that complicated data shall be organized once by human intelligence, put on tape or punched cards, and thereafter be analyzed, recorded, printed out, filed, or otherwise manipulated by machines according to appropriate directions. In the business world this is called integrated data-processing, and the principle is just as applicable to libraries as it is in business. The problem has been that punched-card machines have been designed for business purposes and for statistical data. The necessary transition to the use of such machines for alphabetic and even bibliographic data has now been made successfully in terms both of machine technology and of costs.

Within recent years the International Business Machines Company has produced a simple combination of some of its basic component machines; the resulting product is now called the "Document Writing System." This promises to be as important to libraries, specifically to medium-sized public libraries, as is the computer to big business. In its simplest form—and there are several more complicated variations possible—the Document Writing System consists of an alpha-numeric keypunch machine and an electric typewriter hooked up to the keypunch by cable. Together with a punched-card sorter, these machines rent for about $220 a month, or approximately the salary of one full-time clerical assistant, and many public libraries have access without charge to IBM machines in the offices of the local school system or city government.[4]

The printing card punch can be programmed by snapping into place a card punched on the machine itself. It will read and reproduce on the slave typewriter with designated spacing the words or figures punched into cards and fed into the machine automatically and at high speeds. These cards can be prepared initially on the very same machine by any office girl with appropriate but minimum training. For example, let us suppose that a given library has put on punched cards all the necessary information for a union list of periodical holdings of all local libraries. These cards can be automatically translated into typing on a hectograph or multilith master or on a Mimeograph stencil with complete fidelity. Changes in the record of holdings can be noted by making a new card for each title and each library; experience with one local union

list showed that one-third of all entries needed correction each year, but that still left two-thirds undisturbed.

Another example of the potential use of the Document Writing System is to prepare a list of patrons who owe the library more than a given amount of money. This list is needed in the modern decentralized system of otherwise uncontrolled borrower registration. In order to keep such a list current it should be revised frequently and distributed to all service points; a file of punched cards and the Document Writing System meet the requirement. These machines could be made to type automatically a list of the numbers of the transaction cards missing from all those used with a given due date; this is precisely the point at which human error in copying numbers is most likely to occur. There are many other obvious possibilities: order lists of new books, printed catalogs of the library in book form, lists of new accessions, graded lists for teachers, etc. If the Document Writing System were used for bibliographic purposes, circulation control, and office records, it would probably be in use most of an 8-hour day. Additional work could be handled by a second shift and at an increased rental.

The typing machine of the Document Writing System is a new and distinctive device to translate the meaning of the punches to words. Available at a low cost, it is reasonably flexible. The IBM machine generally used to print out punched cards is its accounting machine, a machine able to add, subtract and multiply and, incidentally, also equipped with type bars to print its totals. The result is that you pay a high price to rent the machine just to use its printing mechanism. Furthermore, until

[4] E. M. Ashley recounts the use of IBM cards for a variety of tasks in Miami high-school libraries, as a result of the availability of the machines in the school system (see his "Clerical Automation," *Library Journal*, LXXXII [July, 1957], 1725–29).

recently it was able only to print in one line what was on one card or to print in one line the sum of what was on two or more cards; the Document Writing System can print on one or more lines the content of any one card, according to the directions given it. On the other hand, it is true, the accounting machine is faster, printing a line at a time and 150 lines a minute.

Think of the number of times the same bibliographical information is handled for one book in a public library. First, the title is considered for selection. Then it is ordered. Perhaps a followup is required before it is received and paid for. It is cataloged (author, subject, and title cards, shelf-list card, and book card), listed in new accessions, referred to in various book lists, eventually rebound, and finally discarded or maybe replaced. The data for all these operations cannot likely be telescoped into one punched card; it may take two editions of the card—one with the information available before receipt of the book and a second with information from the book itself. But even if *two* cards are required to replace *several* manual repetitions, the saving is considerable. Furthermore, this automation should be accompanied by higher speeds, greater accuracy in transcription of information, greater convenience (as in making easily possible multiple copies of book-form catalogs), and services not now economically feasible (e.g., complete lists of books in any subject field). Most important, machine punched-card systems are able to absorb considerably heavier workloads with little or no increase in staff, especially as the people who work with them learn their possibilities and become adept in handling them.

There are, of course, shortcomings and limitations to all machines, to punched-card machines in general, and to the Document Writing System in particular. Anyone who expects not to have breakdowns and not to make mistakes will be disillusioned earlier rather than later. The single most important lesson that business firms have learned in using computers is also one which libraries will have to learn in using punched cards. The use of these machines creates not simply a *better* way of doing things; it is a *different* way of doing things. This means that the job in question should be analyzed into its basic elements and the procedure for doing the job be reconsidered in the light of the strengths and weaknesses of the machine system. For example, if you insist on catalog cards that look as they do at present—not as they have always looked, be it noted—then punched-card machines are not for you. But if you accept the principle of the unit card and of the cumulative features of the Wilson Company indexes, then punched-card machines give you a flexibility and a mechanism previously unavailable to the individual medium-sized library. An example of punched-card contributions to indexing is the permuted title index to chemical literature now being produced by the Chemical Abstracts Service. It is not just another list or catalog. Instead it incorporates a new and different approach made practical by the use of machine punched cards.

The punched card is to libraries what automation is to the modern factory. Beyond such simple machines as those in the Document Writing System lie computers—and some of our large libraries are already planning to skip the punched-card stage and go directly to computers.[5] Special libraries in business and industry are already well embarked on the use of computers and punched cards for the storage and retrieval of both bibliographic information and other data. But for medium-sized public libraries this is not likely to be feasible in our lifetime. This means that most of the possible use of machines for the storage and retrieval of information is also out of reach of these smaller libraries—not the storage and retrieval of bibliographic data on their own holdings but of such material as was put on tape for the library exhibit of the Century 21 Seattle Fair. It would be enough, however, for our generation if medium-sized public libraries were fully to exploit the possibilities of punched cards and their manipulation by electronic machines. The Library of Congress card of the future may be a punched card instead of (or as well as) a printed card. Many interesting and important developments in bibliographical controls using punched cards and computers that are going on in larger libraries and in special libraries in time will undoubtedly have implications for medium-sized public libraries.

GENERAL CONSIDERATIONS

All the main types of machines that have been reviewed here are of par-

[5] "A complete tab operation is not a good intermediary step between manual and automated systems, as decisions not compatible with computer based systems frequently must be made in order to make a tab system work" (Louis A. Schultheiss and Don S. Culbertson, "Applications of Advanced Data Processing Techniques to University Library Procedures: A Study for the University of Illinois at Congress Circle, Chicago," Part I: "The Report" (Chicago: University of Illinois, 1962), p. 102 (Mimeographed). Published as *Advanced Data Processing in the University Library* (New York: Scarecrow Press, 1962).

ticular value to the size of library under discussion. Though they cost money to buy and to operate, they are at least available. This cannot always be said of necessary personnel. The cost of machines, furthermore, comes from a non-sensitive portion of the budget, for in my experience new money for equipment is usually available even when money for additional positions or higher salaries is not. Machines, in addition, add new potentialities to existing services. Nothing takes the place of being able to punch the button on a reader-printer and of giving a patron a life-size reprint of a story from the microfilm of a newspaper. In a world geared to science and to the mass handling of goods and services, the role of machines in libraries and all other occupations is sure to increase steadily and indefinitely.

There are at least two main discernible effects of such machines and technological developments on the personnel situation now and in the future of medium-sized public libraries. One is that they will certainly make easier the performance of routine operations. The wet pick-up lightens the load of the custodial staff; the photocopier saves the time of a typist in making another needed copy of a letter; a card-sorter replaces the arranging by hand of numbered transaction cards. What happens to this time and energy is at least in part a question for the library administrator to answer, but it is a social good for people not to have to do what machines can do for them as well or better. A second main effect of the use of such machines is to complicate the situation of the work supervisor and professional librarian. Not only must he add to his own competence the ability to operate or at least understand the operation of these machines, but he must also take machine methods into account for his calculations of work methods, costs, and possible alternative ways of doing things. This complication is not necessarily bad, but it makes the task of the librarian that much more difficult. (If it is any consolation to the librarian of the medium-sized public library to know it, the task of those employed in larger libraries is likely to be even more complicated.)

Specifically, I do not envisage a completely mechanized or automated library to be practical or realistic in the foreseeable future. But machines now available at a reasonable cost and not commonly used by libraries are capable of measurably reducing the load of routine work and of expanding the service possibilities of medium-sized public libraries. As a result they will probably not reduce the need for professional librarians but may even increase it.

It is easy to become fascinated with machines for their own sake. It is just as easy but less obvious to resist the introduction of machines because of the unsettling effects they are likely to have on established habits of work. If libraries were private businesses, they would measure the cost of machines and their value in terms of net profits. A possible alternative method of deciding when and how far to go in using machines is to be found in the advice of the professional staff of a library, after they have had a chance to visit and observe machine installations, and to study them. In general, public libraries have been cautious in adopting machines. On the other hand, the rate of abandonment of machine methods by libraries which do adopt them is very low.

Sometimes a given library proposes to wait until one perfect method of circulation, card reproduction, book ordering, or other process has been evolved, and not adopt one method now only to replace it later with a better one. Unfortunately, there is not likely ever to be one perfect method of doing anything. You have to work with machines, whether photocharging, punched-card sorters, or bookmobile generators, in order to appreciate their strong and weak points. Far faster and sounder progress will be made by an individual library if it begins to use machines in a small way and then explores future possibilities, based on its actual experience and current needs. You must understand machines to utilize them, and you must have experience with them to understand them.

To this endorsement of the future possibilities of technological development some cautions should be added. First, the introduction of machines is not likely to show any appreciable saving of present staff. Most medium-sized public libraries already have so few employees that the presence of new machines simply relieves one or more people to turn to other badly needed functions, and during the familiarization process new machines require more, not less, staff time. On the other hand, the great advantage of machines—and the basis by which their total potential contribution should be judged—is their likelihood of handling an ever greater workload with little or no appreciable increase in staff. There is a parallel in the telephone industry. In the 1920's the dial system was introduced not in order to reduce the number of operators but in order to handle with greater speed and fewer errors the greatly increased number of telephone calls expected in the future. Today there are more telephone operators than when dial telephones were introduced, but I am not so sure we will be able to secure even more catalogers in the future than we have now.

A second caution in the use of machines by libraries is that it is better to eliminate a process or routine—if such is indicated—than simply to mechanize it. In other words not everything that libraries do should be continued, even if a machine can be bought to do it. I can suggest some things that medium-sized public libraries ought to abandon —such as centralized registration, the slipping of books, the taking of inventories, etc. Maybe you do not agree that *these* specific jobs should be discontinued, but the point is that before any job or task is mechanized it should be critically reviewed as to the necessity for its continued performance. Of *all* the methods of work simplification, *elimination* is the most effective.

On the other hand and by the same token, the use of new machines in libraries opens up many more possible analyses and jobs than when hand systems are used. Before you succumb to the temptation to use a new machine in such a manner, be sure the job or information is really needed. For example, borrower registration files with their wealth of personal information about the registrants lure one to attempt all kinds of analyses. Coding such information on punched cards makes refined analysis possible. But this adds a new load on the machine and a new burden to the staff. The question is, "To what purpose?" Certainly there is only an obscure relation between registration records and circulation records (not to speak of reading and its effect). Machine effort as well as staff effort should not be wasted on fruitless tasks.

Finally, it is clear that there are now many possible machines with applications for public libraries, and even more are sure to arise in the future. As a result it is necessary, inevitable, and desirable that some experimentation be done by some libraries using various machines and various methods. Controlled experimentation would be even more desirable, as by the Library Technology Project. In any case, the results of such trials should be reported in the literature and made available to the profession. We need in some journal or other a method of reporting the best and most appropriate machines and other technological developments from business, industry, education, government, and the experience of other types of institutions.[6] Individual librarians must find the time to read one or more journals in this area (e.g., *Administrative Management,* monthly at $4.00 a year), to visit trade fairs, and to seek out promising machines and relevant applications. Libraries have usually followed in the wake of the developments of society generally, and cultural lag would seem to place public libraries today about on the threshold of the machine age.

AN ESTIMATE OF THE FUTURE

No one can say with certainty that some new invention just ahead will not revolutionize printing (and libraries)

[6] "Goods and Gadgets" in the *ALA Bulletin* and "Products and Equipment" in the *Library Journal* do not supply the type of information needed. More to the point are Jean Casten's "Technical Topics," in the Pennsylvania Library Association *Bulletin* since the Fall, 1961 issue, and the annual reports of the former Committee on Library Supplies and Equipment of the Pacific Northwest Library Association.

as drastically as did Gutenberg's invention more than five hundred years ago. But based on what we know today and can reasonably project into the near future, at least three main lines of influence can be described.

On the one hand—as a sort of minimal estimate of the future place of technological developments in medium-sized public libraries—there is the strong probability that change will come slowly and in small steps, and that it will be resisted for all sorts of reasons and by all sorts of people, including patrons, librarians, and trustees. Even the title of this paper as given to me suggests that behind the façade of rosy promise is the harsh reality of lack of performance or at least at an efficient or economical level. Of all the public libraries in America today that serve from 25,000 to 150,000 people each, no more than about 10 per cent have utilized to the full the opportunities for service, the resources of their staff members, the values and attractions of books, the potential for informal education, the facilities of their physical plant, and the utilization of presently existing machines that are within their budget. If they were operated as profit-making enterprises, many of the rest of them would fail and deservedly so. It takes no cynical observer of this scene to realize that extensive or widespread utilization of new methods or new machines is not likely to occur as a general rule or in any reasonably short time.

Not that this conservatism is necessarily bad, but it simply underlines the fact that new developments in machine applications are likely to be adopted slowly. And this conservatism is reinforced by the natural difficulties of understanding technical aspects of even mildly complicated apparatus and by the conflicting claims of competing manufacturers and alternative devices. There is no royal road to the solution of this problem. Each individual librarian who feels his responsibility in this regard must study the subject as well as he can, observe actual installations in business firms and other libraries, and begin in a small way rather than by trying to evolve at once a full and final answer.

A second main line of influence—what may be regarded as the middle line of probable development—is composed of those libraries that are or have been active in the development and exploitation of modern technology —the public libraries of Montclair, New Jersey; Gary, Indiana; Racine, Wisconsin; Decatur, Illinois; and the North Central Regional Library at Wenatchee, Washington, to name a few in this specific size class. Every one of these libraries has made mistakes in its quest for the best answer to an operating problem, but the profession has benefited by those mistakes. No one can ever foresee and guard against all possible errors and miscalculations. Aerospace scientists lose a few million dollars worth of rockets on an engineering error, and go back to the drawing boards to make an improved model. Librarians, however, tend to feel that mistakes in one actual installation outweigh all possible theoretical advantages of a new method or a new machine. Science does not eliminate all error but acts so as best to profit from it.

At one time public libraries typically had their books on closed shelves, and patrons were expected to fill out call slips for books they wanted and to present these to an attendant at a wicket. We smile at this method of operation, which so clearly could not cope with the tremendous demands of today and which needlessly reduced the service potential of the library. Yet when open access was first proposed, it was hotly fought on both practical and theoretical grounds. And it took more than a few libraries' hesitant experiences with open access to convince the others to follow. It may be that in our generation the great issue will be whether considerably more extensive use of machines in public libraries will or will not do more harm than good— harm in dehumanizing library service and removing the personal element, and good in coping with ever larger workloads and relieving people of routine mental and physical chores. The libraries that pioneer in this area deserve credit for trying.

The third, or maximum line of, influence in the future consists of the overwhelming and ever accelerating pace of scientific change and technological development. We live in the midst of wonders so immense that we cannot grasp their significance. The electron microscope and the cyclotron plunge man into the mysteries of the composition of matter; space capsules take him into whole new realms never before accessible, with fantastic possibilities just ahead of interstellar travel. And most of these developments have occurred in our lifetime; 90 per cent of all the scientists the world has ever had are alive today. I do not see how any institution can fail to be affected—and drastically—by the impact of these changes. Look at some of the common marvels of today—television, plastics,

transistors, frozen foods, antibiotics— and wonder not whether libraries will be affected by this stream of change and development but whether indeed they will be swept away and completely displaced by some other type of agency.

When one sees a giant four-color printing press, or a machine for automatically setting bowling pins, or a device for programmed learning, it is hard to believe that somehow the problems and needs of public libraries are such that science and technology have only minor applications. There is no theoretical difficulty; the problem is simply to find the money to pay people with adequate technical knowledge to take the time to make the practical application. Specifically in the field of punched cards, and related techniques, the number of applications has grown immeasurably. Magazine publishers use them for subscription renewal notices. Book publishers use them for inventory control. Banks use magnetic ink characters on millions of checks to replace hand sorting and accounting by machine methods. Most short-answer type national examinations now use machine-readable answer sheets. None of these applications was necessarily inevitable, obvious, or even easy. The library applications of this same type will have their share of technical difficulties too, but will probably also have their share of rewards in time.

In a broader sense than I have previously considered here, the question of the application of technology to medium-sized public libraries can be interpreted as applying to the spirit of disciplined inquiry and of the scientific method in general. Granted that science cannot provide one with values, purposes, or goals, it is nonetheless true that many persons reject the proposition that science has any discernible or worthwhile contribution to make to librarianship. There are still those who claim that librarianship is an art or at most a humanistic discipline and is not a science or even susceptible to scientific study. There is no known evidence as to the opinions on this point of the librarians in medium-sized public libraries, but not many of them have recorded or shown in fact any considerable use of the scientific method of study. Yet every year many of them make decisions and spend money on projects whose utility and effectiveness are largely unknown.

To give two examples: If a medium-sized public library introduces a film or record collection, do these services reach new strata of the population served or are they used primarily by the people who already make heavy use of the book services of the library? In 1949, Berelson estimated that the latter answer was more nearly correct, based on what a sample of people said they would probably do.[7] By now we ought to have some empirical evidence on the point, but none has ever come to my attention. In another field, consider the time-honored device of a summer reading club for children, which is probably found in most public libraries of this size group. If these programs have an educational value, it is presumably in what they contribute to the retention of the children's reading skills. No study has been made on this specific

[7] B. Berelson, *The Library's Public* ("A Report of the Public Library Inquiry" [New York: Columbia University Press, 1949]), pp. 79–82.

point, but surely if such values are found to hold true then it should be possible to ascertain whether it is better to emphasize the quantity of books so read or some "qualitative" factor such as variety of subject matter or appropriateness of reading level.

To paraphrase Toynbee's hypothesis in his *Study of History*, an institution will grow and flourish or decline and perish depending on the ability and willingness of those who control that institution to modify the means by which they control it so as successfully to meet the challenge problems of their day. Unfortunately it is only by hindsight—and sometimes not even then—that we can clearly identify what *are* the challenge problems of a given age, and which *are* the successful or effective responses. Both of these are matters of judgment, in any current scene, but the great point is that the ruling elite must be able and willing to change its techniques of operation. However, if a challenge problem is not met and solved, it will tend to recur in different ways and in ever more pressing form until it is solved or until it overwhelms the institution.

In our day and age crucial problems are posed for public libraries by the information explosion and the need for ever greater understanding by ever more people of ever more complex matters. All possible means of solving these problems should be examined and tried, and I believe that one important avenue of exploration should be based on the scientific method of inquiry in general and on the possible applications of machines in particular.

ROLE OF THE MEDIUM-SIZED PUBLIC LIBRARY
IN THE "SYSTEM" (NEW YORK)

JEAN L. CONNOR

IT HAS been said that "the elephant was invented so that four blind men could stand around feeling one and then give opinions."[1] If the elephant had not been invented, a public library system might have served as well, for it, too, has many parts and is provocative of many opinions.

A public library system organized on a federated or co-operative, non-consolidated basis, is still seemingly considered a beast of some rarity and those who have actually handled this curious animal are frequently asked to relate their impressions. Although in the classic story there are always four blind men, the opinions I report draw upon correspondence with twenty-eight librarians of medium-sized libraries participating in library systems in New York State and a few who are not.

The first thing I should make clear is that such a thing as a public library system does actually exist. In New York State, we have twenty-two, of which only the three in New York City are consolidated systems. As of June, 1962, 92 per cent of the state's population and 94 per cent of the area are served by these twenty-two systems. Systems serve every county—forty-one entirely and twenty-one partially. The organizational work has been almost entirely completed; the twenty-two systems cover the whole state. No library is a member of a system unless it wishes to be. Membership is not forced but is voluntarily voted upon by each local library's board of trustees. Thus, this membership of 594 libraries reflects the faith of trustees and librarians in the library-system concept, the co-operative approach to improved public library service.

There are thirty-eight libraries in New York State that serve populations of between 30,000 and 150,000 (see Table 1). Of these, thirty-two are members of library systems and only six are not. Their membership is quite diverse; they belong to fifteen systems in the state. (There is a marked concentration of medium-sized libraries on Long Island. Eleven are members of the Nassau System.) Apart from the three New York City systems, only four do not have medium-sized libraries as members.[2] It is clear, then, that the medium-sized library has found a place for itself within the public library system development that has gained ground so rapidly in New York State in the past four years. And they have an important role to play, for, outside of New York City, the medium-sized libraries serve approximately 20 per cent of the population of the state.

SYSTEM ORGANIZATION

There are three principal types of library systems in New York State—the

---

[1] Henry Morgan, "The Phoenix Nest," *Saturday Review* (July 7, 1962), p. 115.

[2] Two systems that lack communities of 30,000 population within their service area are Clinton-Essex-Franklin and Southern Adirondack. Two systems that have no medium-sized libraries but do have both smaller and larger libraries are Onondaga and Mohawk Valley.

consolidated, the federated, and the co-operative. All are recognized under our State aid to library systems law,[3] a law that has achieved success in part because it permits diversity of organizational patterns. The consolidated pattern, where one library board is responsible for the entire library program, staff, books, and budget, is the familiar city library and branches pattern. This does not appeal to medium-sized and

[3] New York State Education Law 272–73.

small libraries, which wish to band together for improved services and strengthened resources, without losing their separate corporate identity. In New York, no medium-sized library is a member of a consolidated system; all are members of either federated or co-operative systems. Federated systems are organized by vote of the county board of supervisors, who establish the system and appoint the system board of trustees.

TABLE 1

RELATION OF MEDIUM-SIZED PUBLIC LIBRARIES
TO SYSTEMS IN NEW YORK

	Population Served, 1960	System Membership
Albany	129,726	Upper Hudson
Niagara Falls	102,394	Nioga
Utica	100,410	Non-member
Elmira	98,706	Chemung-Southern Tier
New Rochelle	76,812	Westchester
Mount Vernon	76,010	Westchester
Binghamton	75,941	Four County
Troy	67,492	Upper Hudson
Williamsville	62,837	Erie
East Meadow	58,935	Nassau
Levittown	57,709	Nassau
Irondequoit	55,337	Pioneer (Monroe)
Rome	51,646	Mid-York
Massapequa	51,195	Nassau
White Plains	50,485	Non-member
Smithtown	50,347	Non-member
Great Neck	50,000	Non-member
Greece	48,670	Pioneer (Monroe)
Elmont and Stewart	46,000	Nassau
Hicksville	46,000	Nassau
Jamestown	41,818	Chautauqua-Cattaraugus
Farmingdale	41,236	Nassau
Valley Stream	38,629	Nassau
Poughkeepsie	38,330	Mid-Hudson
Patchogue	37,929	Suffolk
Oceanside	35,500	Nassau
Auburn	35,249	Finger Lakes
Pleasantville	34,955	Westchester
Hempstead	34,641	Nassau
Freeport	34,419	Nassau
West Seneca	33,644	Erie
Eastchester	33,613	Westchester
Watertown	33,306	North Country
Newburgh	32,400	Ramapo-Catskill
Long Beach	31,000	Non-member
North Tonawanda	31,000	Non-member
Lockport	30,500	Nioga
Lawrence	30,200	Nassau

Unlike the board of a consolidated system, the board in a federated system does *not* manage all units in the system. Instead, the system's trustees and chief librarian serve as coordinators and planners. In a federated system, the system's board is *not* responsible for and does *not* control the operations of the member libraries of the system. The board of trustees of each participating library continues to be charged with full responsibility for the selection of its staff, books and other library materials, for its program and hours of library service, for the provision and maintenance of library buildings, for the preparation of annual budget requests.[4]

The same description applies to the co-operative systems, except that they are organized by association of the libraries themselves after vote of the respective boards of trustees; no action of the county board of supervisors is required. The co-operative library system, first authorized under an amendment to our law in 1958, has become the dominant organizational pattern. All new library systems organized since 1958 have been of the co-operative type.[5] The essential point about both co-operative and federated systems is that the libraries are joined together by a service plan, by contracts, but they do not vote themselves out of separate existence. Through the co-operative pattern, the local library is able to retain the benefits of individualism and local autonomy, plus gaining the benefits of larger regional resources and services. We could not have achieved almost complete system coverage of the state if this had not been

[4] University of the State of New York, State Education Department, *Report of the Commissioner of Education's Committee on Public Library Service, 1957* (Albany, 1958), p. 33.

[5] The Chemung-Southern Tier System is a "mixed type," formed by contract between two smaller systems, one federated and one co-operative. The Pioneer System is also a "mixed type," but is usually classified as federated.

so. I suspect that the medium-sized libraries would have been the strongest resisters to any movement that would have involved losing their individual status. The New York State system law has provided a way for all libraries, of whatever size, to work together.

STATE AID

The library systems in New York receive state aid, based on a formula which gives attention to three basic factors—the population served, the size of the area served, the number of counties served—plus an additional incentive reimbursal factor based on the amount spent for books, periodicals, and binding. The basic per capita grant is $0.30, but the other factors in the formula bring the state aid to an average of about $0.60 per capita. The state-aid formula is premised on a goal of $3.00 per capita, of which the state would contribute 20 per cent. The total state appropriation for aid to libraries for the year beginning April 1, 1962, is $9.4 million. The amount spent in the past year was, in round figures, $8.5 million. This money goes from the state to the systems. It is not given as cash grants to individual libraries, which are responsible for their own local budgets. It is money for system services, to be spent for a plan of co-operative activity that could not be undertaken by each library working alone. The system board of trustees submits a plan of service for the approval of the state commissioner of education and, upon his approval, the system receives an annual grant based on the formula described.

There is one other type of aid of particular significance to library systems that do not have large libraries, where the medium-sized library becomes, relatively, the big library. The law provides that systems that lack a central library containing a collection of at least 100,000 adult non-fiction volumes shall receive grants of books, on a four to one matching basis over a ten-year period.[6] In order that each system contain at least one strong core collection of books for reference and educational purposes, this book aid is given to build up the non-fiction collection of the central library for system-wide use. Of the thirty-two medium-sized libraries participating in library systems, seventeen receive book grants-in-aid through this feature of the state aid to library systems law.[7] (In some systems, more than one library in a system serves as a reference center and shares in the book aid.) These books become an additional resource for inter-library loan. They are a compensating factor in the systems that lack large

[6] Regulations of the Commissioner of Education, No. 101a, and New York State Education Law, sec. 273:1.

[7] Seventeen medium-sized libraries serving 30,000–150,000 population, receiving book grants-in-aid to build up their collection of non-fiction are (1) Nassau System: Freeport, Hempstead, East Meadow, Levittown, and Hewlett-Woodmere; (2) Nioga: Niagara Falls and Lockport; (3) Chemung-Southern Tier: Elmira; (4) Four County: Binghamton; (5) Upper Hudson: Albany; (6) Mid-York: Rome; (7) Suffolk: Huntington and Patchogue; (8) Chautauqua-Cattaraugus: Jamestown; (9) Mid-Hudson: Poughkeepsie; (10) North Country: Ogdensburg; (11) Ramapo-Catskill: Newburgh.

Other libraries outside of this population group receiving book aid under this state program are: (1) Mohawk Valley: Schenectady, 152,896 population; (2) Finger Lakes: Ithaca, 28,799 population; (3) Ramapo-Catskill: Middletown, 23,409 population; (4) Chautauqua-Cattaraugus: Olean, 21,739 population; (5) Clinton-Essex-Franklin: Plattsburgh, 20,172 population; (6) Southern Adirondack: Glens Falls, 18,580 population; (7) North Country: Massena, 17,730 population; (8) Southern Tier: Corning, 17,085 population.

city library collections such as exist in Buffalo and Rochester, and this feature of the 1958 state-aid law was a factor in winning acceptance of the system concept by the medium-sized libraries.

THE TYPICAL LIBRARY SYSTEM

The profile of a typical library system in New York State looks like this:

1. It is organized in such a way as to preserve the independence of the member libraries.

2. There is a regional board of trustees governing the system's co-operative services and providing co-ordination of library planning on a broad areawide basis.

3. The system has a headquarters staff, distinct from that of the central library, whose main task is to give supporting services to the member libraries.

4. The system receives state aid to provide services to the member libraries.

5. The local or member libraries are locally financed.

6. The population served by the system usually totals over 300,000.

7. The system usually serves more than one county.

8. The system usually has many member libraries; the approximate average is thirty.

9. The system is relatively new; it has been operating only about three years (of the thirty-two medium-sized libraries participating in systems, only five belonged to a system before 1958).[8]

10. Every system has a central library collection, which, if needed, is being built up to adequacy through state book grants.

Here then, is a brief portrait of a library system. Like the elephant, it is large. We may next ask: What can it do?

The services offered by library sys-

[8] New York has had a state aid to systems law since 1950, but the real breakthrough came in 1958 when new legislation authorized co-operative systems and increased the state aid. Medium-sized libraries belonging to systems before 1958 were Elmira, Irondequoit, Watertown, Williamsville, and West Seneca.

tems are diverse, but within the varying service patterns certain core programs emerge which are particularly significant to the medium-sized public library.

NEEDS OF MEDIUM-SIZED LIBRARIES

To see how the medium-sized library fits into the system, a brief description of the characteristics of our medium-sized libraries is essential. As pointed out earlier, seventeen of our medium-sized libraries actually serve as the "big libraries" of their system area. With the exception of Nassau, Suffolk, and Westchester counties, contiguous to New York City, the medium-sized library is usually pretty much in a class by itself, serving as leader and pivot in the system. In the metropolitan suburban counties, the situation is different; the medium-sized libraries are more numerous and some of them think of themselves as "small." (Of course any extension librarian who has worked with rural libraries could speedily correct that idea!)

I asked the medium-sized libraries in systems what were the three major problems that faced them in the next two years. The problems checked by the most libraries in order of frequency, were as follows:

1. Need to recruit additional professional personnel (17)
2. Need to extend service to growing community (16)
3. Need to build and improve book collection (14)

Choices selected by less than a majority were:

4. Need to secure more adequate physical quarters (13)
5. Need to increase local tax support (11)
6. Need to improve public relations "image" in the community (7)
7. Need to educate board of trustees (2)

8. Other (4) (Of these, two mentioned need for improved salary scale.)

With a nationwide shortage of personnel, the large number indicating "need to recruit additional librarians" might have been anticipated. Probably the reason for the high score for the "need to extend service to growing community" is that two out of three of these libraries are located in rapidly growing communities, where "keeping up" is a real problem.

It is interesting to look at these problems in relation to the system's potential. Not all are within the library system's province; the system cannot help solve all problems equally, or to the same degree. The problem of securing a better building, for example, or of establishing new branches, is a local problem. There is no magic in the system; it cannot do everything. There are dangers in overexpectation, in believing that, somehow once the system is operating, everything will be easy, even as there are dangers in underestimating what can be accomplished through the co-operative approach.

What can library systems do for the medium-sized public library? The services provided by library systems are numerous, including interlibrary loan, loan of films, consultant services, centralized processing, reference service, public relations programs, rotating book collections, aid in book selection and workshops.

Services—interlibrary loan.—Interlibrary loan is by far the most popular and most valuable service, as rated by the member libraries themselves. It is both a mandated system service[9] and a popular one. The success of this

---

[9] *Regulations of the Commissioner of Education.*

feature—the right of a reader to draw upon the book resources of all libraries in the system without charge on the same basis as a reader in the local library—seems to indicate that the first step in provision of system services should be the offering of interlibrary loan service on an organized basis.

Interlibrary loan is not new. What *is* new is a service that is publicized regionally as a reader's right. It is not just a special courtesy. Also new or expanded in the development of inter-library loan services are union catalogs or author-finding lists in each of the systems.[10] Particularly helpful has been the introduction of delivery service, on a regular schedule, to speed the flow of loans between libraries. Interlibrary requests are cleared in each system and, if not filled, are forwarded to the State Library by teletype. (Teletype use is growing.)

Interlibrary loan does benefit medium-sized libraries, not just small libraries. The number of volumes borrowed by twenty-eight medium-sized system libraries increased 46 per cent in the three-year period 1958–61.[11] Medium-sized libraries report almost unanimously that they make very frequent use of interlibrary loan, and we know from experience in the older systems that such use will grow over the years.

Medium-sized libraries also serve as resource centers for loan to other libraries, and this too increases with system membership. The number of volumes loaned by twenty-eight medi-

um-sized system member libraries increased 157 per cent in the three-year period 1958–61.[12] Even so, when the number of books borrowed and loaned by medium-sized libraries is compared, there is no marked imbalance. In 1961 the medium-sized system libraries borrowed approximately 20,000 volumes and loaned approximately 24,000.

System membership is thus seen to speed up the flow of books to readers over a region, utilizing existing book collections to benefit everyone. Asked whether system membership had caused a serious drain on their own library's resources as a result of this area-wide use, three out of four of the medium-sized libraries said "No." And it is anticipated that, after several more years of building up the central library collection through state aid, an equitable balance will be achieved for all.

The total result of system interlibrary loan service, delivery service, and union catalogs has been a positive one. Three out of four librarians report definite improvement in reader services as a result of system membership.[13]

It might be noted that the systems have generally undertaken broadened borrowers' privileges, over and beyond interlibrary loan, on a gradual basis. The right of the reader to have direct access to any library in the system without charge is a part of the five-year plan of every system; today it exists in three out of five medium-sized libraries. They report it a valuable service. Less common and more controversial

[10] Nassau, Westchester, and Suffolk had union catalogs operated by their county library associations before the organization of the library system.

[11] The median percentage of change for the same period for six non-member libraries was −34 per cent.

[12] Median percentage of change during the same period for six non-member libraries was −32 per cent.

[13] In answer to the question, "Has system membership enabled you to improve reader services?" twenty-one medium-sized system libraries replied "yes," two hedged and only two replied "no."

are the development of a uniform borrower's card, and the privilege of return of books to any library in the system. New systems need time to work out new patterns of sharing.

Film service.—A service that received a remarkably high score in popularity among the medium-sized libraries was the loan of films by the system. An enlarged and expanded film service was desired, more so than any other service. This is because film service fits admirably the definition of system function in the ALA standards: "A library system provides the various joint services and activities which enable a group of smaller library units to achieve, together, standards which would be beyond the reach of each individually."[14] Second, films are relatively new to libraries. Librarians are therefore more quick to recognize their need, not only for shared resources, but for consultant services. About half of the medium-sized libraries are in systems with audio-visual specialists,[15] and the present and potential value of help they can give is ranked high.

Consultant services.—All systems have consultant services. Some have specialized consultants in children's, young adult, and adult services. In other systems, general consultants serve as Jacks-of-all-trades. As might be expected, use of the children's consultants is more frequently reported than the use of the other specialists. Some consultant or field services are used relatively infrequently, and a few libraries stated flatly they do not use the system

consultant services at all. Apparently, acceptance of consultant help takes time. Some of the difficulties encountered are:

Need for consultants who are new to extension work to develop knowledge of the region equal to that of local directors, and to develop consultant skills that establish an easy human relationship, within which the consultant role can be achieved.

Need for member libraries to recognize their own need for improvement.

Need of the system to devote its largest proportion of consultant time to the more pressing needs of the small libraries, those lacking professional help.

Need for more time to make the results of the "educational role" of the system visible.[16]

Need of system staff to devote a heavy percentage of time in the first years to services other than field work.

It is clear that system consultants working with medium-sized libraries will need a great deal of tact, patience, and exceptional skill in their chosen specialties if they are to win full confidence and build a successful program. Unlike consolidated library systems, where a direct supervisory relationship prevails all down the line, consultants must learn to lead by suggestion, never to command.

At the moment, most system consultant services to medium-sized libraries are new and a harmony of recognized need and service rendered is yet to be fully achieved.

Centralized processing.—Another system service, offered to four out of five of these libraries, is centralized purchasing and processing of books. Within the next year, almost all will have such service available to them without cost.

[14] *Public Library Service, a Guide to Evaluation, with Minimum Standards* (Chicago: American Library Association, 1956), p. 16.

[15] Systems that have audio-visual specialists at this time are Nassau, Westchester, and North Country.

[16] In answer to the question, "Has system membership been a positive factor in in-service training of your staff?" only eight of the libraries answered "Yes" and twenty answered "No."

This is something they want and use. Its potential value to them is rated high, but their comments also indicated that the quality of centralized processing, as presently offered, should be improved. Probably in no other system service is efficiency more critical. Small libraries have lacked professional cataloging, and their standards for judging system service are less exacting than those of the medium-sized library. Systems need the highest level of organizational and technical skill in the development of processing service. Speed is particularly important. Where these conditions are met, the local library benefits greatly in saving time, space, and money, all of which can be devoted to other services.

Rotating collections.—The system provision of rotating collections of books, or book pools, as a supplementary book resource is noted in almost all cases. The difficulty here is in tailoring this service, usually developed to fit the needs of the small library, to the richer collections of the medium-sized library. More specialized collections would seem to be the answer; for example, books in foreign languages were cited as useful when provided from a central pool.

Reference service.—A core concept in the philosophy of public library systems is the provision of reference service, or, as the ALA Standards put it, "A library system should have a plan for referral of information inquiries from community libraries to the central agency when they cannot be answered locally."[17] Such a plan for referral exists in every system. The natural center for reference service is the largest library in the system. Research indicates that a library system, from the point of view of the library user, is only as good (in depth) as the level of service in its strongest library.[18] In fourteen of the twenty-two library systems of the state, there are no large libraries;[19] the largest available in twelve of these might be classified as medium-sized, and two as small libraries.

It is obvious, then, that the quality of reference service in most library systems rests upon the quality of reference service available in the medium-sized library. The improvement of that service is not one that can be accomplished by the system alone. It takes teamwork, for we are dealing with an interdependent program, where the adequacy of the central library reference staff, building, and finance, the plan for intrasystem referral, system services to the central library, and supplementary reference service and book aid from the state, all play a part. Some of these are human problems, as are all problems in teamwork. The development of a library system demands new patterns of cooperation, and it is sometimes easier to share "things" than to share a "service." New York State has made a good beginning in solving the problem of adequate *book* resources for reference service through its book aid feature in the state-aid program and the State Library's backstopping services. More work will be needed and considerable

[17] *Public Library Service*, p. 17.

[18] University of the State of New York, State Education Department, *Report of the Commissioner of Education's Committee on Public Library Service, 1957* (Albany, 1958), pp. 113, 117.

[19] Systems that have large central libraries are New York City, Brooklyn, Queens, Pioneer (Rochester), Erie (Buffalo), Onondaga (Syracuse), and Mohawk Valley (Schenectady).

ingenuity if the problem of adequate reference *staff* for area-wide service is to be licked.

One important question to be worked out is the extent to which the system headquarters (as distinguished from the central library over which it has no administrative control) should attempt to provide supplementary reference service to member libraries. The thorny questions of finance and equity and level of local adequacy in the provision of a regional service present other challenges that one does not solve in the beginning years of a library system.

There are, of course, limits to the level of reference service that the medium-sized library can provide. The New York State system structure provides the means through which all readers have a channel to informational services. But an additional step must be taken; a capstone to the structure is yet to be provided.

For a full solution to the problem of reference service at the highest or research level, new systems utilizing the resources of college, university, and special libraries will be needed, as in the plan proposed by the Commissioner's Committee on Reference and Research Library Resources. With the consummation of this plan, the user will be put in touch with the total resources of all libraries of all types in the state.

Aid in book selection.—A major service offered by the library systems is aid in book selection through provision of review copies, shared book selection tools, check lists, and regular book review meetings. In the federated and co-operative systems of our state, book selection is a local responsibility, exer-

cised by each local library. The system has no supervisory control over what the local libraries purchase, and since the money for local book purchase comes from local sources local autonomy is fully protected. The only role of the system is an educational one— teaching good book selection practice and providing information upon which sound decisions can be reached.

Problem areas in the system's service to libraries in the field of book selection include: (1) Difficulty in finding centrally located meeting places within reasonable distance for all members and in scheduling meetings convenient to all. (2) Difficulty in working out timing of selection; medium-sized libraries want more material evaluated and want it more quickly than do the smaller.

On the positive side, system directors report that the personnel of medium-sized libraries have actively participated in book discussion and other system meetings, setting an example and helping to foster the co-operative spirit.

Services summarized.—There are other services that the medium-sized library would like from the system— frequently requested is assistance in public relations, the provision of promotional tools, such as book lists, posters, etc. Care is needed so that the system public relations program is oriented toward promoting library service through the local outlets—the member libraries—rather than publicizing the system center itself.

In summary, interlibrary loan, films, rotating book collections, centralized processing, consultant services, aid in book selection, and reference service are the basic elements in system programs, and the medium-sized library benefits from all of them.

As a measure of present success and potential for the future, when the libraries that are members of systems were asked which of twenty-nine system services they would recommend eliminating, only two votes were cast,[20] which really means that practically no one wants to eliminate anything! When asked which of these twenty-nine services should be enlarged in scope or further emphasized, all but two services were mentioned by some of the libraries,[21] with the highest priorities going to films, the union catalog, interlibrary loan, and centralized processing. So for almost every service offered, there is someone who says, "More, please." The real problem is thus to further improve the services presently started, to deepen the gains that have already been made, and to achieve that quality of service that can only be achieved in the maturity of system development.

NON-SYSTEM MEMBERS

The question may well be asked: If the systems have succeeded so well, what about the non-members? Why do they not join?

The six remaining medium-sized libraries not in systems were asked, and they gave the following reasons:[22]

1. Lack of building space to handle increased use (2)
2. Fear that reference load would be too great (2)

3. Did not feel it equitable to extend use of local resources to persons outside the community (2)
4. Fear of dictation by the state (2)
5. Lack of direct financial aid from the state to the library
6. Fear that local support would be cut
7. Saw no advantages
8. Questioned quality of centralized processing

When asked what were the major problems they faced in the next two years, three stated: "need to recruit additional professional personnel." This was the same problem given top priority by the member libraries. It will be interesting to study this a few years hence. I venture to predict that, if these libraries continue to stay out of systems, they will find it more and more difficult to recruit new personnel. The oncoming professional librarian, given a choice between working in a member or non-member library, may be expected to choose a system member because of the professional association and help that can be his within the regional structure.

All the fears mentioned have been raised before in the organizational stages of library systems. The only real answer is that the success of systems in meeting the needs of the member libraries must speak for itself.

The holdout libraries will be interested in the following comparisons:

1. Circulation has gone up in both member and non-member libraries, but the percentage of increase is somewhat greater in the member libraries.[23]
2. Local tax support has gone up in both member and non-member libraries. There is a difference, however, in the rate of increase. Non-system members are having to raise local

[20] One vote was cast to eliminate special consultant services in the adult field, and one vote was cast to eliminate area reference service through central libraries!

[21] Centralized purchasing of supplies and equipment.

[22] There were four responses out of six polled.

[23] Median percentage of change in circulation, 1958–61, for twenty-eight member libraries, + 19 per cent; for six non-member libraries, + 15 per cent.

taxes faster to keep pace with need, than are system members.[24]

3. Total number of additions to the book stock has risen in member libraries, but has dropped in non-member libraries.[25]

Is local autonomy endangered? When asked, "Has system membership resulted in loss of local autonomy?" twenty-three members said "No," and only three said "Yes." That even those who said "Yes" did not consider the degree of loss serious was indicated by other votes cast by these respondents on the value of services rendered by the system.

Under the New York State plan, the complete autonomy of the local board of trustees to decide on whether their library will join a system has been retained. Perhaps these few remaining holdouts should be treasured rather than censured, as positive proof that our rapid progress in system coverage has been achieved through the democratic process.

SYSTEMS VIEW THE MEDIUM-SIZED LIBRARY

A most interesting and enlightening view of an elephant is that through an elephant's eyes. Accordingly, I asked the system directors themselves about how they viewed their relationship with the medium-sized library. The responses of twelve directors of co-operative or federated library systems in New York State were thoughtful and helpful.

[24] Median percentage of change in income from local tax monies, 1958–61, for twenty-eight member libraries, + 25 per cent; for six non-member libraries, + 38 per cent.

[25] Median percentage of change in additions to the book stock, 1958–61, for twenty-eight member libraries, + 18 per cent; for six non-member libraries, — 15 per cent.

In outlining the problems which they faced in serving medium-sized libraries, they cited the following:

1. Difficulty in gearing book selection meetings and book selection checklists to needs of both the small and medium-sized library. Since small libraries predominate, their needs have come first. Medium-sized libraries are building collections of greater depth and scope and have not been greatly helped by aids prepared for smaller libraries.

2. Difficulty in co-ordinating centralized ordering and processing. The medium-sized libraries order heavily on a prepublication basis, while the small libraries do not. The medium-sized libraries have wanted more elaborate processing than that needed by the small libraries.

3. Difficulty in providing the more specialized consultant services which medium-sized libraries seem to want, and, conversely, difficulty in getting acceptance of consultant service per se because of a climate of complacency.

4. Need to stimulate staff and trustees of medium-sized libraries to long-range planning to meet demands on staff, building, and collection resulting from rapid population growth.

The systems, given time and money, have some ideas on programs they would like to undertake to better meet the needs of the medium-sized libraries. Some of those mentioned were:

1. Provision of specialized consultant services by the systems that do not, for example, have children's or young-adult specialists.

2. Provision of publicity tools, posters, displays, promotional pamphlets, news releases, etc.

3. Assistance in building book collection and staff adequate to meet reference needs of the region.

4. Film and record collections.

The system directors were cognizant of the special contributions that medium-sized libraries have made in system development, greatest, of course, being the comparative strength of the book collection. But their leadership role, past and present, was also cited. The staffs of these libraries may include the only professionals outside of the system headquarters itself. Because of their experience and education, they are often drawn upon for system programs and workshops.

They assist the untrained librarians. They serve on committees. But most valuable of all, as one system director put it, "They provide a good sounding board for the system staff in evaluating system services. They can also give sympathy and encouragement." Here is another system director's perceptive analysis: "I would suspect that it is also good if the medium-sized library were constantly and constructively critical of the system's program."

Thus, the role of the medium-sized library as sounding board and friendly critic can be an invaluable one to system staff, as well as an interesting professional challenge to the directors of the medium-sized libraries. Good communications and harmonious relations between the system and its member libraries are basic to this fruitful interchange.

CONCLUSION

This concludes my report, including the observations of the directors of library systems and the directors of the medium-sized libraries. Like the blind men who handled an elephant, we have had many opinions. They are tentative opinions based on a comparatively short period of experience. And they are the views of librarians. The ultimate test of a library system's success must be that of its impact upon the library user, and for such a report, we must await more research. But on one thing we can all agree: Systems are here to accept and respect.

A final word might be given the directors of medium-sized libraries that are members of library systems. When asked what difference it would make to them if systems did not exist, one answered simply, "disaster" and another said, "Let's not think about that!" To the question, "Do you believe library systems are here to stay?" they all answered "Yes."[26]

We know that not all needs of the medium-sized library can be met by the system. Some are local responsibilities. And some, as has been indicated, may best be met at the state level. It may well be that the program of service to the medium-sized libraries should receive increased attention by the state extension agency. Particularly in those systems where there are only one or two medium-sized libraries, the provision of some of the needed services (for example, specialized consultant services, reference service, co-ordination, and film service) at the state level seems logical—and more possible as the developing system programs relieve the state agency of some of its traditional responsibilities for guidance to the very small libraries.

However we view it, the medium-sized library is in a critical and strategic position in the development of a state-wide pattern of adequate library service. It deserves the attention of its local community and of system and state staff, so that its resources may be fully utilized, its contribution equitably

[26] Of the twenty-eight libraries answering, twenty-six said "Yes" and two did not answer. None said "No."

recompensed. It is increasingly clear that only through a network of service, through some pattern of co-operation and system services, can a medium-sized library hope to do the full job for its readers. A library system opens to every reader a new channel to enlarged book resources and better library service.

I see the future as one in which, there is reason to hope, the problems of system development will gradually give way to the forces of time, patience, persistence, and understanding. The system and medium-sized library together will wish to carefully define goals and engage in continuous joint planning.

It has been said that "the beginnings and ends of man's every great enterprise are untidy."[27] The development of systems is not an easy task or a quick one. We in New York are still in that "untidy" state of beginning— but we believe that the beginnings we have made are truly the beginnings of a "great enterprise," and that through establishment of our systems we have laid the base for progress in the years ahead.

[27] Sebastian DeGrazia, *Of Time, Work and Leisure,* quoted in *New York Times,* June 18, 1962, p. 27.

RESPONSES OF TWENTY-EIGHT OUT OF THIRTY-TWO MEDIUM-SIZED LIBRARIES TO QUESTIONNAIRE ON RELATION OF MEDIUM-SIZED PUBLIC LIBRARY TO A LIBRARY SYSTEM

I. Rate the following services as to the extent of your use of them, their present value and your recommendations.

Service	Services Offered by System		Use of Services, as Now Offered			Value of Present Services, as Now Offered				Potential Value of Service, If Added, Enlarged, or Improved, Would Be				Recommendations on Present Services: Service Should Be			
	Service Is Not Offered	Service Is Offered	Use Service Frequently	Use Service Infrequently	Do Not Use Service	Very Valuable Service	Valuable Service	Of Little Value	Of No Value	Very Valuable Service	Valuable Service	Of Little Value	Of No Value	Improved in Quality or Efficiency	Enlarged in Scope or Further Emphasized	Curtailed or De-emphasized	Eliminated
1. Direct access to any library	11	17	8	6		6	8		1	6	6			1	5		
2. Uniform borrowers card	22	6	4		1	3	1			16	5	2		1	1		
3. Interlibrary loan		28	25	2		20	5			1	1			2	13		
4. Return of books to any library	21	7	3	3	1	3	3	2		6	6	2	1		3	1	
5. Rotating collections	10	18	6	5	4	5	5	2		8	8	2	1	3	9		
6. Pool collection of books	17	11	2	3	2	3	4	2	2	8	5	1	1	3	6	1	
7. Films loaned	4	24	13	7		10	11	1	2	11	6			3	18		
8. 16 mm. projectors loaned	17	11	1	5	3	3	2	2		3	4	3	1	1	5	1	
9. Phonograph records loaned	18	10	1	5	3	1	5	2		2	6		1		6	1	
10. Record players loaned	27	1		4	1	3		1	1	2	4		1	1	1		
11. Union catalog or location file		28	18	4	1	16	4	3	1	12	3			7	10		
12. General consultant service	7	21	2	13	2	5	8	3		7	5	4		3	6	1	
13. Special consultant service, adult	9	19		8	3	1	3	5	2	2	6	4		2	4	2	
14. Special consultant service, young adult	11	17	6	7	5	4	6	3		3	6	4			7	3	1
15. Special consultant service, children's	7	21	10	6	2	8	6	3		4	6	4		2	4	1	
16. Special consultant service, audio-visual	13	15	5	10	2	5	8	2		4	9	2		1	10		
17. Special consultant service, reference	14	14	5	6	2	5	4	1	1	4	7	3		1	8		
18. Special consultant service, public relations	17	11	1	8	2	2	2	3	1	5	6	3	1	2	6	2	
19. Aid in book selection—tools, check lists	4	24	11	8		8	6	3	1	5	6	3	1	2	6	2	
20. Aid in book selection—book discussion meetings	3	25	12	6	2	11	7	2		7	8	1	1	3	7	1	
21. Workshops and program meetings for librarians	12	16	4	6		7	5	2		11	5	1		3	9		
22. Workshops and program meetings for clerical staff	23	5	2	1	1	2	2		1	8	4		1	3	5		
23. Workshops and program meetings for trustees	18	10	3	5	2	4	4	2		9	3	2		9	7	2	
24. Central purchasing—books	6	22	15	1		11	4			12	4	3	1		4	2	
25. Central purchasing—supplies	20	8	3	1		2	1			5	5	3			5		
26. Central purchasing—equipment and furniture	27	1	1	1		1	1			5	2	3	2		5		
27. Central processing	5	3	16	1	3	12	4	3	1	12	3			11	5	2	
28. Reference service (through central library[ies])	6	22	7	5	1	7	5	1		8	2	2		1	11		1
29. Reference service (through system center)	14	14	3	4	3	3	3	1	1	7	2	2	1	4	5		

THE MEDIUM-SIZED PUBLIC LIBRARY: IN
RETROSPECT AND PROSPECT

LEON CARNOVSKY

WITHIN the present century, and particularly within the last fifty years, two significant trends have been evident in the American population; both have contributed to thrusting the medium-sized community into a position of greater prominence. One trend is the flight from the city to the suburb; the other is the decline of the rural population, with a concomitant increase in the population of the urban community. These trends are readily documented in the 1960 United States Census and in the Hauser-Taitel analyses recently published in *Library Trends*.[1] Consider the cities between 25,000 and 100,000 in population; in 1950 we had 379 of them, and in 1960 the number had increased to 633. Ten years ago cities in this size class accounted for 11.7 per cent of the total population; today the percentage is 16.1.

We are all familiar with these trends; we need only add that, whereas cities of more than 500,000, in 1950, contained 17.6 per cent of the population, in 1960 the proportion had dropped to 15.9 per cent, and the decline was particularly marked in the cities of more than 1,000,000. But much more striking is the flight *to* the city from the country. Farm population dropped from 30,000,000 in 1940 to about 20,000,000

in 1960 (actually, only 16,000,000 by new census definitions). In order to put the medium-sized community into perspective in view of these population shifts, let me read a passage from the Hauser-Taitel analysis:

The relative importance of the various size groups within urban territory changed during the decade. It was the cities of intermediate size, populations between 10,000 and 100,000, which increased in relative importance. They contained less than 31 per cent of the urban population in 1950, but more than 37 per cent in 1960. Most of this growth was at the expense of our larger cities, particularly those with populations of 1,000,000 or more.[2]

These figures underscore the fact that the medium-sized community has a long future ahead of it. Like all our political units, it is subject to continual change, and its institutions will be called upon to react to such change. The same, of course, applies to the large city and to the rural area. For the large city the pressure of metropolitanism will increasingly be felt; how this will affect the library remains to be seen, though we are already aware of the ever growing dependence on such libraries by non-resident populations. For the rural area, already burdened by too low density of population to make local library provision feasible, the future outlook is even darker; as Hauser and Taitel tell us: "Farm population may be expected to decline further in view of mechanization developments and productivity increases. By 1980 the farm population may include no more than 12 million

[1] Frank L. Schick (ed.), *The Future of Library Service: Demographic Aspects and Implications* (Urbana: Graduate School of Library Science, University of Illinois, 1962). Reprinted from *Library Trends*, X (July, 1961), 6–70, and X (October, 1961), 71–286.

[2] *Ibid.*, p. 28.

129

persons as compared with 16 million in 1960."[3] This means, I believe, that the state library and its extension service must play a larger role in serving them, or that a different kind of library unit must be created to bring service to them.

My assignment is to present a somewhat generalized summary of much that has already been said, plus some commentary suggested by the several papers. In this summary I shall pay particular attention to book collections and book selection principles, censorship, service to children and young people, personnel, finance, state and federal aid, and the "systems" concept of library organization.

First, book collections. This topic was covered by Cushman in connection with adult reading and by Smith in his emphasis on the less frequently demanded but highly important type of book. Cushman in particular had a good deal to say about paperbacks and their implications for library acquisition policy. Here he raised the possibility of saturation purchase, to relieve the problem of numerous calls for the same book at one time. I wonder, however, if this is the only, or the most useful, application of the paperback revolution that we can make. Heavy use of individual titles is likely to be affected by two considerations: the immediate demand for best sellers, and the requirements of school assignments. By the time best sellers reach paperback status they are, with few exceptions such as *Rise and Fall of the Third Reich, To Kill a Mockingbird,* etc., no longer best sellers. However, is it not proper to raise the point that once even such titles are issued in paperback, the patrons

[3] *Ibid.,* p. 29.

may be expected to purchase them themselves? I wonder if saturation buying is an appropriate solution.

This leads me to another aspect of the paperback: what it has done to commercial book distribution in the medium-sized community and the implications for the public library. As we know, the paperback has brought an enormous number of books and a wide variety of titles to the attention of everyone. No longer is the conventional bookstore the sole or even the major distributor. Heretofore, such stores existed only in the larger cities; if serious books were to be found in the medium-sized community, the public library had to be the source. Today, good books, paperbound and inexpensive, are available, if not to everyone, certainly to an infinitely larger number of people. If *To Kill a Mockingbird* can be bought for fifty cents, is it really necessary for the public library to compete with the commercial enterprise by buying numerous copies? I am aware, of course, that the paper-bounds most heavily provided through local commercial channels are not of this caliber, and are more likely to be of a quality which the library never acquired at all. Still, as Houle points out in his masterly analysis of the paperback: "A few leading trade-book and university publishers had already realized that the gap between the mass paperbacks and the hard-bound books might be filled by books which could retail in the one- to four-dollar bracket, which could justify that price by their superior content, design, paper, and binding, and which could be supported economically by the sale of far fewer copies than was possible for the mass paperbacks. Moreover, the sales of serious titles in the cheaper series showed that a substantial public for such books was developing."[4]

The book reader today, thanks to the omnipresence of paperbacks, has a wealth of material available that was inconceivable a quarter-century ago. For much of his reading he may face the choice of borrowing a book from the library without charge, or buying it. If he chooses the library, he must be sure to come when it is open, limit his loan period to a couple of weeks, make another trip to return it, and risk a fine if it is overdue—all this on the assumption that the library not only has the book but that someone has not beaten him to it. Alternatively, he might walk to the corner, pay fifty cents, and the book is his. It is foolish to deplore his preference for the second alternative, and even more foolish to attempt to dissuade him from it. This, however, is only part of the story. Many, perhaps most, of the quality paperbacks will simply not be available, and if he wants titles such as, say, Newman's *World of Mathematics,* or even Willa Cather's *O Pioneers!* he may have to depend on his public library. Perhaps the implication to be noted is that book funds may be used to buy precisely the kind of book which is not readily available elsewhere, to provide the kind of entertainment, to say nothing of the kind of information and substance, which is not easily purchasable or obtainable.

After all, however, the paperback is nothing more than a different physical form of book; the basic question that all librarians must face is one of book selection. On this point Cushman and

Smith were quite definite, both stressing the *positive* aspects of book provision. A book is important as it contributes to the elevation of reading taste, or to the educational, intellectual, or cultural process. Smith seems particularly emphatic on this point; if I were to characterize his philosophy of public librarianship in one word it would be "involvement." The library, he believes, has the obligation to become involved in community affairs—involved actively and positively—and this requires decisions not only or even primarily concerning a book's popularity or limited appeal but concerning its significance. Choices must inevitably be made, and he unequivocally casts his vote for the significant.

The problem of significance is an extremely difficult one. Even without going into the question of what the word means (significant for whom? for what purpose? at what time?), we cannot expect the librarian—or anyone else for that matter—to make sound judgments in the limitless areas in which books are written. This is difficult enough even in adult fiction, and the professional critics are not invariably helpful. A recent article in the *New Yorker* reports that when Scott Fitzgerald's *Tender Is the Night* was published, it was condemned as a failure; today it is selling at the rate of a half-million a year. Can anyone question the obligation of the public library to make this "failure" available? This is not to question the Cushman and Smith emphasis on the necessity of literary standards in book selection and in reader guidance, but only to suggest that it must be supplemented by an awareness of public demand, and of the utility of even less distinguished books in library collections—an aware-

[4] Cyril O. Houle, "Two Revolutions and Their Consequences: The Paperback in Our Contemporary Culture," *ALA Bulletin,* LVI (July–August, 1962), 656.

ness which I am sure both these librarians amply reflect in their own institutions.

What more can be said about censorship? The ALA "Freedom To Read" statement is forthright and unexceptionable; it says exactly what we all believe, as librarians and as American citizens. On the other hand, we have the Fiske report, which confirms what all of us suspected and many have experienced —that in spite of our vigorous protestations, overt and covert censorship is one of the facts of life. The seriousness of the problem will certainly vary from one community to another, depending on all sorts of influences and factors which are external to the librarian himself—among others, the mentality and courage of the library board, the power and attitudes of local persons and groups, the interest and sophistication of the community. Is this problem more serious in the medium-sized than in the large library? As a hypothesis, I suggest that the smaller the community, the greater affinity its residents have for their library, and the greater concern they will have about its policies and practices. And consequently the more conscious they will be of their prerogative to tell the librarian what he may or may not do. Here, I believe, is the real censorship problem—not the failure of the librarian to believe in the freedom to read, but the unwillingness of others to accept the First Amendment to the Constitution. (Perhaps I give the librarian too much credit; certainly in the illustration cited by Smith, if the rejection of the Russian gift pamphlets "to foreclose controversy," was a librarian's decision, it was little less than shameful. However, even here, before a too-easy condemnation on my part from the

ivory tower where I live, I should like to know more about the influence of library boards and community groups which may have forced such censorship.)

I suspect, however, that most of our troubles in this area spring from the contemporary focus on sex literature. I have become increasingly uncomfortable over the glib distinction between "literature" on the one hand and "dirt for dirt's sake" on the other; but fortunately we have the courts to help us. What is dirt to one reader becomes a book of "redeeming social importance," whatever *that* means, to another—and a Supreme Court Justice at that. Having myself read *Tropic of Cancer,* I doubt if I have been either besmirched or redeemed by it; and to assume that others would be harmed by reading it is arrogant. The late Professor Zechariah Chafee of Harvard has written: "The great interest in free speech should be sacrificed only when the interest in public safety is really imperiled, and not . . . when it is barely conceivable that it may be slightly affected."[5] And only this year the Massachusetts Supreme Court, in lifting the ban on *Tropic of Cancer,* stated:

We think that the First Amendment protects material which has value because of ideas, news, artistic, literary or scientific attributes. If the appeal of material to adults is not predominantly prurient, adults cannot be denied the material.

When the public risks of suppressing ideas are weighed against the risks of permitting their circulation, the guarantees of the First Amendment must be given controlling effect.

It is not the function of judges to serve as arbiters of taste. Within broad limits, each writer . . . is entitled to determine such matters for himself, even if the result is as dull,

[5] *Free Speech in the United States* (Cambridge, Mass.: Harvard University Press, 1948), p. 35.

dreary and offensive as the writer of this opinion finds almost all of "Tropic."[6]

Certainly when the courts themselves have ruled that a book is admissible to publication and sale, librarians and their trustees should be loath to frustrate the demand for it.

Next, a word or two about another aspect of censorship—though one which does not ordinarily come under that opprobrious term. This is the neglect by the medium-sized library of poetry, drama, the experimental in literature—in short, the kind of book, whether imaginative or factual, that is rarely acquired. Again both Smith and Cushman referred to this, both of them deploring the extreme conservatism of our book-selection practices. Their point is well taken; it is precisely this kind of book that must find its audience through the public library, or there may be no audience. But the dilemma in which this places the medium-sized library is too obvious to need emphasis; with its limitations in funds and personnel, it cannot risk being so far out of touch as to lose public contacts altogether. The solution must lie in such administrative innovations as the area extension trans-county program described by Smith, the systems described by Miss Connor, and in numerous co-operative arrangements engineered by two or more libraries, with or without the stimulus of state financial aid. But let us be perfectly clear on this point: as long as popularity remains the key to book selection, the door will remain closed to the provision of the unusual book. Even many of our state libraries, with the entire state as a potential audience, are woefully weak in their provision of truly

significant, up-to-date book collections. Money of course is part of the answer, but only part; until we recognize the obligation to provide such books, more money will lead to the purchase of more books of the conventional kind. Such evidence as we have on acquisitions of small and medium-sized libraries bears out this observation of Dan Lacy:

> Take a really important book (one not a sensational best-seller or book-club choice), a good, solid, thoughtful book on any of the great economic or political or foreign policy issues on which our whole future depends. The odds will be that in three-fourths of the counties in the United States there is not now and never has been a copy of the particular book in any book store or library; that it has never been reviewed or mentioned in a newspaper published there; it probably has not been mentioned on any radio or television program heard there, or reviewed in any magazine subscribed to by more than a handful of people who live in those counties. That is the true censorship which really restricts the freedom of information in the United States.[7]

SERVICE TO CHILDREN AND YOUNG PEOPLE

Library service to children and young people continues to be a strong element in the program of the medium-sized library, and with good reason. Everything happening in our society seems to contribute to increased library demands from and obligations to the young. First, take the population pattern. In 1950 the five- to thirteen-year-olds numbered about 22,000,000; the fourteen- to seventeen-year-olds, nearly 8,500,000; or, combined, 30,725,000. In 1960, the combined totals amounted to 43,780,000—an increase of 42 per cent. By 1970 the totals are expected to

---

[6] Quoted in *Publishers' Weekly*, CLXXXII (July 30, 1962), 30.

[7] *First Annual Freedom of Information Conference, University of Missouri, December 11–12, 1958: Speeches* (Columbia: University of Missouri, 1959), p. 25.

be nearly 53,000,000, and by 1980, about 59,000,000. In short, the population between five and seventeen years of age in 1980 will be some 92 per cent more than it was in 1950. This increase will of course be reflected in school enrolment; the 1980 enrolment is expected to be 105 per cent greater than the 1950 enrolment. In a period of thirty years we shall more than double our elementary and high-school attendance.[8]

Aside from this sheer numerical increase we may anticipate a much more intensive use of reading materials. The scientific and technological events since the war have led to an accelerated interest in learning more about them—an interest likely to have a tremendous impact on library use and on the character of library collections for young people. In this area, I suspect, we have a somewhat different problem than in the adult collection. Whereas in the adult collection we could at least suggest the possibility of foregoing certain kinds of books, such as titles available in cheap paper-back or books of inferior quality in favor of the seminal and significant, in the children's collection the alternative is not so easy. This is because we have always aimed at quality for its own sake in children's book selection, and there is little to surrender. As I see it, then, we shall have to continue to provide the kinds of books for children and young people that we now do, only we shall need vastly more of them, and in still greater variety. Considering the population and school growth, I do not see how this can be avoided.

At this point it will be useful to look at circulation patterns. First, what has happened to over-all library circulation in the last twenty years? Second, what

has happened to the circulation of books for children? For the first, we have some evidence in the Index of Library Circulation regularly published in the *ALA Bulletin*. Based on the median of a sample of thirty-eight libraries in cities over 25,000, total circulation in 1961 was 24 per cent higher than it was in 1939. This is not surprising in view of population growth, to cite only one contributing factor. What *is* surprising is that, whereas juvenile circulation constituted 33 per cent of the total 1939 circulation in the median library, it accounted for 49 per cent in 1961. The same thing shows up in the more extensive compilations of the Library Services Branch, already reported by Winger. The over-all circulation in 1960 from 822 libraries consisted of 52 per cent plus for children's books and 48 per cent for adult. Anyone who thinks that the coming of school libraries means the end of children's work in public libraries had better think twice.

This is not to derogate the school library movement in any sense. It is definitely on the march, and we may anticipate a vast increase both in the number and quality of elementary and high-school libraries. When this comes we shall have to consider very carefully whether a changed emphasis or different focus is desirable for work with children and young people in public libraries. We are a long way from the saturation point in children's reading, and the coming of new and better school libraries may, and probably will, result in tapping a new group of readers, without diminishing dependence on public libraries. In fact, I think it altogether possible that each type of library will tend to spur use of the other, with increased reading from both.

[8] *The Future of Library Service,* pp. 33–34.

PERSONNEL

It will be noted that at least one topic of surpassing importance has been omitted from the program: personnel. This was not an oversight. It was omitted because we did not see the necessity of stressing once more the facts with which we are all familiar—shortages, poor preparation, improper utilization of professional staff, etc. Of course these are serious problems, but rehearsing them will neither solve them nor reduce their annoyance. In point of fact, however, the topic has not escaped notice, and in several papers it has come in for attention, either explicitly or by implication. Goldhor's paper in particular, though focused on hardware, carries profound implications for the number and kinds of people we shall need, and the way we use them. One clear implication is that perhaps even more than machines to help us in bookkeeping and housekeeping and to enable the maintenance of ever more sophisticated records, we need to take a hard look at the records we now keep to see how useful they are. If we need more people to keep more records or to do things that can be dispensed with, the solution may lie in eliminating or simplifying such records and activities, and in assigning simple tasks to persons who are able to do simple tasks fully as competently as highly trained persons. We all know that cataloging of foreign literature, maps, rare books, serials, government documents, corporate publications, etc., is no job for a tyro, but in all honesty we should ask whether such materials loom large in a small or medium-sized library. Is it really so difficult to train a reasonably intelligent person who has never seen a library school to catalog the fiction and ordinary non-fiction that make up the overwhelming proportion of such acquisitions—especially when Wilson and Library of Congress cards are already available? I have seen such use made of bright college graduates in large libraries; I suggest that it is feasible for smaller libraries as well.

Whether or not we choose to follow this path, I believe we shall be forced to it, or something like it, in the future. Winger reminded us that in 1961 only 387 accredited library-school graduates took positions in public libraries of all kinds; and there were more than 387 vacancies in 315 libraries alone! I remind you that there are more than eight thousand public libraries in the entire country. Consider the alternatives. We might have more library schools, accredited and non-accredited; or we might have larger enrolments in existing and future library schools. These would certainly help, but the facts are that for a long time neither alternative has been particularly effective, and the need for librarians remains desperate. Remember that public libraries compete with academic, school, special, and government libraries for good people, and the needs of such libraries are multiplying at a much faster rate than the library schools can hope to match. We hardly need to be reminded of what is in store for high schools and colleges when the expanded elementary-school population hits them. The medium-sized public library will continue to look to library schools for personnel relief, but its lot is more likely to be frustration than fulfilment.

Goldhor was not sanguine about the possibility of reducing the number of staff members in medium-sized libraries, since the staffs are already small. This is undoubtedly true, but I believe that the more important aspect is the proper utilization of the staff we have. What tasks need doing that do not get done because of financial or personnel limitations? My guess is that these are not record-keeping or routine matters, but rather such things as reader guidance, development of book collections, public relations, co-operative enterprises with other institutions, contacts with community groups and with schools, etc. If we could shift our trained people from the routines on which so many of them are engaged to such activities which seem properly professional, we might find that the problem of shortages is really not to be solved by finding more people but rather by using the people we now have more effectively.

FINANCE

This conception of the role and future of the medium-sized library has been based on what is taking place in society at large. We have looked at the library against a background of population trends and movements, educational developments, and community expectations. It is high time that we turned to a consideration of that by which the library rises or falls, grows or remains stagnant, namely, money.

Of course it is true that library income has increased appreciably in the last two decades, an increase stimulated in part by shrinking purchasing power of the dollar, in part by the competition for personnel and the need for higher salaries, and in part by expanded local programs—more branches, more personnel, more books and services. How much farther we can go in obtaining enlarged revenues is a moot question, and the answer lies only partially in the ability of the library to demonstrate how much better it could do its job if more funds were available. As Leland has pointed out, most libraries—and

communities—are saddled by the inefficient and out-dated property tax; whatever virtues it may have had at one time, its yield at present is not nearly great enough to subsidize the activities of government. The library itself, its income frequently limited to the yield of a special earmarked tax on property, will undoubtedly find itself seriously hampered unless the tax limitations written into state legislation are raised appreciably—and along with this goes the willingness of the local community to impose the higher tax rate—or unless it finds other sources of support to supplement or replace the tax on property. One such source is the general fund of the municipality; this, as we have seen (Leland), has grown enormously—from $914 million in 1902 to $37.5 *billion* in 1960! But along with this increase, and indeed responsible for it, is the elaborate multiplication in local responsibilities—schools, highways, police and fire protection, welfare activities, and the like. It would be well worth learning whether libraries with earmarked taxes have fared better than those which are required to take their chances along with other local government enterprises in obtaining money from the general fund. Many librarians have long preferred the earmarked tax regardless of its yield, because it assured a definite income, and they have feared, probably with reason, that in an open contest for a share of the general fund they would be less well provided for. But it seems certain that the improved services suggested by several speakers can come about only as more money is available; and the prospects for more money, at least from local sources, do not seem particularly rosy.

Do they seem any rosier from nonlocal sources? Here we must consider the states and the federal government. State grants have been made to local libraries to assist them in times of distress and also to enable them to extend service to areas beyond their political jurisdiction. Certainly aid to medium-sized public libraries has not been extensive. As Leland has pointed out, in 1957 only thirteen states made grants to local units, and some of these units were very large cities. In view of the financial burdens that all states carry, they are not likely to welcome the invitation to participate in activities that have traditionally been considered of purely local concern. Nevertheless, this is something they will have to consider. Particularly under the impact of the Library Services Act we are recognizing the desirability, not to say the necessity, of library service to areas unable to provide it for themselves; we have yet to come to grips with the problem of urban areas whose libraries are handicapped by inadequate local resources. At this point the analogy with state grants for education is worth noting. In 1902 the states appropriated $45 million for education; the comparable figure in 1960 was $5 billion. Plainly, educational needs have made a tremendous appeal to state legislatures and they have generously responded. Cannot the concept of education be extended to libraries as well? As far back as 1928, in a notable decision Missouri Supreme Court Justice White laid down the dictum that "Education is not limited to schools and it is within the control of the General Assembly, in the exercise of the state's police powers, to provide for other educational agencies."[9] There is of course nothing revolutionary in this concept, and states have had the right to appropriate funds

[9] *Carpenter* v. *St. Louis,* 2 S.W. (2d) 713 (1928); 318 Mo. 870 (1928).

for local libraries whenever they chose to do so. But because the language of the Court so strongly emphasizes the library as an educational agency, it points the way for greater participation by the state in library matters—just as it does for the schools.

Thus far, when we have looked to the state for relief it has been primarily to help the rural population. Some states have held out the promise of financial assistance if counties or regions would organize a library system; on the other hand, as we know, the states have done relatively little for the already functioning, self-contained local library. Whether or not they will do more in future remains to be seen, but the portents are good. The Library Services Act, with its matching requirements, led to substantial appropriations for the improvement of rural library service; if we should succeed in getting a Library Services Act to aid urban libraries, may we not also anticipate a greater degree of state participation than we have experienced in the past? With this question before us, let us turn to a consideration of federal action in the public library field.

I need not review the history and provisions of the Library Services Act, especially since Leland has already reported its major provisions. We need no longer wonder if this first step was also the last step, in spite of its built-in five-year limitation. Ten years ago, when this Act came up for a hearing before the Subcommittee of the House Committee on Education and Labor, Mr. Greenwood of New York asked Dr. McGrath, then Commissioner of Education:

"How do you feel about this being a permanent hand-out from the Federal Government to the States? Do you think that would be taken care of; that once the stimulation was used, eventually, perhaps in 5 years or so, the States would be able to take over this program without help from the Federal Government? . . . Do you think there would be a tendency to let the States go on their own eventually, provided stimulation is provided by the Federal Government?"

Dr. McGrath: "I think, Mr. Greenwood, that there might be some agitation for grants to the library systems of the States, but I do not contemplate that in this legislation. This bill provides a terminal date at the end of 5 years. The real purpose of the bill, as I understand it, is to do the very reverse of the thing which you are raising the question about. The purpose of the bill is to stimulate State and local communities to provide their own library facilities for their own citizens. . . . The purpose of this legislation is to show communities what a real library service can do for their citizens in the hope that they then—the citizens of those communities—having seen the benefits of good library service will be willing to pay only $1.50 a head to provide such minimum facilities."

Mr. Greenwood: "Thank you."[10]

The renewal of the Act for a second five-year period is a tribute in part to a successful lobby in Washington but much more to the success of the Act itself. In its brief existence it made so strong an impact that the agitation for its continuance had a true grass-roots impetus. Now we are about to witness a campaign for library assistance of truly imaginative proportions. On May 21, 1962, Representatives Bailey of West Virginia and Miller of California introduced an amendment to the Library Services Act,[11] subsequently supported by congressmen from sixteen other states,[12] which called for the following provisions:

I. Public Libraries. Removal of the population limitation of 10,000, and increasing the authorization to $20,000,000 annually to be allotted on a matching basis to the States for the further extension of public library services to areas without such services or with inadequate services.

II. Public School Libraries. Authorization of $30,000,000 annually for matching grants to State educational agencies to assist in library service in public elementary and secondary schools.

III. Institutions of Higher Education. Authorization of $10,000,000 annually for matching grants to institutions of higher education.

IV. Library Training Institutes. Authorization of $7,500,000 for fiscal 1963 and $10,-000,000 for each of the four succeeding fiscal years for short-term or regular session institutes for training to improve the qualifications of librarians and student-librarians.

This is quite an amendment: from $7.5 million annually, which the Act now authorizes, to some $70 million annually! And for libraries of all types and sizes. Of course, it is a long way from introducing a bill to getting the presidential signature to getting appropriations; but even if the amounts are whittled down considerably it is a matter of no small significance that such a bill should be introduced at all. And when we realize that the states will be expected to match much of the appropriation—if we reach that point—we may anticipate a mighty transformation in the shape of the library of the future. It is not too early for every librarian to plan the future of his own institution —to ask himself what needs doing and exactly how he would use such funds as may be coming to him through state and federal aid. How do the population trends described for the nation as a whole apply in his own community? What are the prospects for increased school enrolment locally, and what are likely to be their impact on the library?

---

[10] Hearings before a Subcommittee of the Committee on Education and Labor, House of Representatives, on H.R. 5195, "A Bill To Promote the Further Development of Public Library Service in Rural Areas" (82d Cong., 2d sess.; April 1 and 2, 1952), p. 9.

[11] H.R. 11823 (87th Cong., 2d sess.).

[12] As of July 31, 1962.

What are the weaknesses in his collection, and specifically how might they be eliminated? What programs of adult education seem necessary and feasible? What services not provided at present are blocked by financial shortcomings? I suggest that the very process of planning may lead to the initiation of some programs that do not depend on external financing, or that may be substituted for others which may be less necessary but which are carried on because they always have been. It is sobering to realize that even after several years of preparation for the present Library Services Act many states were not yet ready with plans for utilizing the funds made available to them when the legislation was enacted. We should take warning from this; hard thinking about the specifics of library operations, planning their improvement, expansion, or even elimination, should be the charge to every librarian.

The power of state aid to effect changes in the pattern of public library service has impressively been demonstrated in New York. Here we had no small contributions to enable the purchase of a few more books, but a bold and imaginative program that has given a vigorous forward thrust to the realization of the concept of state-wide library service. All the elements were present to militate against this achievement: strong, locally entrenched libraries fearful of losing their independence and autonomy, apprehension at state interference, an already heavily taxed citizenry, a large state debt. All the elements, that is, except indifference. Thanks to the leadership of the New York Library Association and of intelligent and far-sighted librarians, trustees, and citizens at large, the state has provided generously and effectively; New

York today stands as a model of what such leadership may accomplish.

As Miss Connor has indicated, the key to success has been the flexibility which permitted the advantages of consolidation but without the surrender of autonomy. Thus it is that no medium-sized library in the state gave up anything; through federation and co-operation they all gained stature, and their communities were the beneficiaries. The results in reader benefits are already impressive. We have frequently been told that not only could a library not afford the purchase of the less popular book, but if it were acquired it would remain unused. Miss Connor's evidence suggests the opposite; between 1958 and 1961 the medium-sized libraries that were system members increased their interlibrary loans by an average of 46 per cent. To me this means that a potential interest in books beyond the holdings of the autonomous library existed, and when such books were available, as they were through the system, they were called for. And the increase in loans to other libraries in the system amounted to 157 per cent. Such interlibrary loans, on the other hand, tended to *decrease* in number in the libraries not related to systems.

All this is not to suggest that the New York pattern is readily exportable to all other states. Some may be too small, others too poor, still others too indifferent. Still, the basic elements demonstrated in New York may be applied elsewhere, even though the administrative structure may vary. It may well be that in some places the solution may lie in developing much greater strength at the state level, with direct dependence by local libraries upon state library collections to compensate for local inadequacies. After all, interlibrary loan is not new. Also, a much more active interlibrary co-operation on an informal basis must inevitably redound to the benefit of everyone. Through interlibrary co-operation the medium-sized library has the opportunity of achieving many of the advantages which have been so amply demonstrated in New York, without involving the risk that New York faces if the state legislature some time in future were to decide that it could not or would not continue the elaborate financing to which it is now committed. This does not seem imminent, though it remains a possibility. Far from even harboring such a thought, the New York people are moving toward a much more elaborate scheme of state aid, emphasizing the needs of students, scholars, and research specialists. It will be interesting to follow the progress of this movement, and to see how the small and medium-sized public libraries are related to it.

STANDARDS

Finally, a word about standards. Winger in his paper used two different bench marks as criteria against which to measure the medium-sized library. One was the set of elements proposed by Lowell Martin as comprising the essentials of library service: (1) a book collection providing significant literature on personal and social problems; (2) assistance by specialists in the technical and guidance functions; and (3) organization to facilitate use. All these, as stated in this condensed form, are admittedly vague, and before they can be used to measure the quality of any library they need considerable spelling out. Such spelling out was, in fact, undertaken by Martin in his doctoral dissertation, and to some degree it is reflected in the *second* bench mark employed by Winger—the standards incorporated in *Public Library Service to America*. But these standards were formulated with a minimum service population of 100,000 in view, and thus should not be literally applied to libraries serving less than this number. So we are faced with this fact: Of the 8,190 public libraries and library systems in the United States, only 254 serve populations of 100,000 or more. Our present "systems" standards are therefore only partially applicable to nearly 8,000 libraries, and of course the greatest number of libraries arbitrarily defined as medium-sized fall in this group.

Under the circumstances we have tended to fall back on the old 1942 *Post-war Standards for Public Libraries,* but these are so badly out of date as to be largely inapplicable today. At least, however, they had the virtue of recognizing the reality of the libraries we all know; perhaps we need something comparable to fit today's conditions. This is not to belittle the current standards, but simply to recognize them for what they are and to warn against their misapplication. In its lofty aspirations, and in the pattern suggested for book collections, personnel, and services, *Public Library Service to America* sets a goal worth striving for though never attained.

CONCLUSION

If these are not the best of times, neither are they the worst. But good or bad, we must take them as they are, adapting ourselves and our institutions to them, hopefully trying in some minute way to improve them. It is a challenge that cries for response. In their own way, libraries contribute their mite to such improvement and to ushering in the light of a new day.

THE CONTRIBUTORS TO THIS VOLUME

LEON CARNOVSKY: for biographical information see the *Library Quarterly*, I (1931), 476; XII (1942), 763; XX (1950), 44; XXI (1951), 299; XXIII (1953), 297; XXV (1955), 398; and XXIX (1959), 56. Mr. Carnovsky was managing editor of the *Library Quarterly* from 1944 to 1961. In the summer of 1962 he was awarded the Melvil Dewey medal for distinguished contributions to librarianship. In the past year he has been a staff member of the group engaged in surveying the library functions of the states and he is currently a member of the Committee on Accreditation of the American Library Association.

JEAN LOUISE CONNOR: associate library supervisor, Library Extension Division, New York State Education Department, Albany. Born Newton, Iowa; A.B., Middlebury College, 1941; B.L.S., Columbia University, 1942. Miss Connor served as a librarian in the Rochester (New York) Public Library from 1942 to 1948 and as a reader's advisor at the White Plains (New York) Public Library from 1948 to 1954. Going to the New York State Education Department as senior library specialist in 1954, she was appointed to her present position in 1957.

JEROME CUSHMAN: librarian, New Orleans Public Library. Born Chicago, Illinois, in 1914. B.A., Park College, Parkville, Missouri, 1940; B.S.L.S., Louisiana State University, 1941. He served with the Missouri State Library from 1941 to 1946 and as librarian at the Public Library of Salina, Kansas, from 1946 to 1961.

HERBERT GOLDHOR: for biographical information see the *Library Quarterly*, XII (1942), 286; XIII (1943), 246; XVII (1947), 233; XIX (1949), 56; and XXIX (1959), 266. Mr. Goldhor became associate director of the University of Illinois Graduate School of Library Science in 1962. Prior to that, he served for eleven years as librarian of the Evansville (Indiana) and Vanderburgh County Public Library. He has recently published, with

Joseph L. Wheeler, *Practical Administration of Public Libraries* (New York: Harper & Row, 1962).

SIMEON ELBRIDGE LELAND: professor of economics and dean of College of Liberal Arts, Northwestern University since 1946. Born Madison, Indiana, in 1897. A.B., DePauw University, 1918; A.M., University of Kentucky, 1919; Ph.D., University of Chicago, 1926; LL.D., DePauw University, 1947. Since 1933 he has served as a tax adviser and consultant to state, federal, and foreign governments. He is the author of numerous articles and books on government finance. From 1920 to 1928 he was on the faculty of the University of Kentucky (Lexington), and he served on the faculty of the University of Chicago from 1928 to 1946, during the last six years as professor of economics and head of the Department.

FORREST LAIRD MILLS: city librarian, Racine (Wisconsin) Public Library since 1953. Born Helena, Montana, in 1913. B.A., Stanford University, 1935; Certificate of Librarianship, University of California, 1936; M.A., University of Chicago, 1951. He served as librarian at Willamette University, Salem, Oregon, and at Enoch Pratt Free Library, Baltimore, and as assistant professor at Mississippi State College. He is a past president of the Wisconsin Library Association, and he was named Wisconsin Librarian of the Year in 1960.

PETER H. ROSSI: for biographical information see the *Library Quarterly*, XXXI (1961), 402. Mr. Rossi is the coauthor with Robert A. Dentler of *The Politics of Urban Renewal* (New York: Free Press of Glencoe, 1961).

RAY SMITH: librarian, Mason City (Iowa) Public Library since 1957. Born Minneapolis, Minnesota, in 1915. B.A., Hamline University, St. Paul, 1937; M.A. (American Studies), University of Minnesota, 1948; M.A. (Library Science), University of Minnesota, 1957. He has worked in a bookstore, as a truck farmer, and as an instructor in English at the University of Minnesota. He is vice president and president-elect of the Iowa Library Association. His publications include *No Eclipse* (War Poems), (St. Paul: Prometheus Press, 1945); clusters of verse in *Poetry* (Chicago), receiving Guarantors Prize for 1945; articles on modern poets in *Lexicon of Contemporary Literature* (Verlag Herder, Freiburg, 1960); and numerous poems and articles in literary reviews and library journals.

RALPH A. ULVELING: director of the Detroit Public Library. Born Adrian, Minnesota, in 1902. Ph.B., DePaul University, 1922; B.S., Columbia University, 1928; L.H.D. (Honorary), Wayne State University, 1956. He has served as president of the American Library Association, 1945 to 1946; vice-president of the American Association for Adult Education, 1944 to 1945; on the U.S. National Commission for UNESCO, 1946 to 1949; and on the Editorial Advisory Board of the *World Book Encyclopedia* since 1952. He has published numerous articles in educational, architectural, and library periodicals. With Charles M. Mohrhardt he has been library building advisor for libraries in thirteen states on $30 million worth of library building projects.

HOWARD W. WINGER: for biographical information see the *Library Quarterly*, XXVIII (1958), 359. Mr. Winger is an associate professor in the Graduate Library School of the University of Chicago and managing editor of the *Library Quarterly*.